SHALL LICKING COUNTY RAISE A REGIMENT?

THE ROLE OF LICKING COUNTY, OHIO, IN THE AMERICAN CIVIL WAR

Edited & Compiled by

DAN FLEMING

LICKING COUNTY LIBRARY

NEWARK, OHIO

2011

QR Code

http://www.lickingcountylibrary.info

Shall Licking County Raise a Regiment?

Copyright ©2011 The Licking County Library, Newark, Ohio

ISBN 978-0615557472

Although the publisher has made every effort to ensure the accuracy and completeness of the information contained in this book, we assume no responsibility for errors, inaccuracies, omissions, or any inconsistency herein. Any slights of people, places or organizations are unintentional. The information printed herein was obtained from a variety of sources including old books, newspapers, photographs, documents and personal interviews. Due to the historical nature of the subject matter, accuracy is not always certain. Due to the age of many of the photographs, the photographer or copyright-holder often could not be determined.

Cover photo: Cannon in Cedar Hill Cemetery, Newark, Ohio.

Book design by Aaron J. Keirns.

CONTENTS

Contents continued on next page…

ILLUSTRATIONS

ACKNOWLEDGMENTS

The collections of the Licking County Library and the Licking County Genealogical Society were heavily used in producing these stories. In addition, the knowledge and expertise of several individuals proved invaluable time and time again, including Mr. E. Chris Evans, Larry Stevens and Doug Stout, all contributors in their own right. We are truly fortunate to have persons of such caliber to help with this project.

We also wish to thank our proofreader, Louise Whitis, who could look deeper to find obvious and subtle points that the rest of us missed.

Following are the authors included in this volume:

Vera Bagent has volunteered with the Licking County Genealogical Society for over ten years and is the current editor of their newsletter, the *Licking Lantern*. She is married, has two daughters and three grandchildren and has lived in Granville for 42 years.

Elizabeth Bicking is a retired teacher, originally from New England. She has strong interests in history, antiques, music and quilting. She currently volunteers with the Licking County Genealogical Society.

Margaret Brooks is a board member, Program Chairperson and Past President of the Board of Managers of the Granville Historical Society.

Peter J. D'Onofrio, Ph.D., of Reynoldsburg, earned his doctorate in American History with a specialization in the American Civil War. He has been a re-enactor and living historian since 1978 and is currently the president of The Society of Civil War Surgeons and editor of *The Journal of Civil War Medicine.*

E. Chris Evans is a Civil War scholar, relic collector and amateur historian. He frequently portrays General William Tecumseh Sherman and Lt. Leonidas H. Inscho in programs around the state. He is also known for relating the story of the sinking of the Sultana steamship. Chris was the chairman of the Johnny Clem Statue Committee which commissioned the 6-foot bronze statue of Johnny Clem. He has had feature articles published in Civil War journals and was named "Licking County Historian of the Year" in 1997 by the Granville Historical Society.

Dan Fleming is a reference librarian at the Licking County Library. He focuses on local history and is passionate about making it more accessible through organizing, writing and indexing. He edited and was a principle writer for the books, *The Bicentennial History of Licking County, Ohio, 1808-2008* and *Journey through 200 Years.* He also edits the newsletters for the library, the Licking Valley Heritage Society, and the Licking Valley Lions Club, Inc.

Anne Kennedy is a reference librarian at the Licking County Library. She gained an intense interest in the Civil War while attending Gettysburg College. She is also the President of the College Town House Fiber Guild in Licking County.

Emily Larson is Curator of the Sherwood-Davidson House and Office Coordinator for the Licking County Historical Society.

Linda A. Leffel is a Newark native, and was a teacher at John Clem Elementary School for 35 years. She continues to be dedicated to preserving the heritage of John L. Clem. She also enjoys her family and friends, writing, speaking, and serving in various capacities on the Board of Trustees of the Licking County Historical Society, as well as other community organizations.

James P. Lukens is a past president and board member of the Licking County Historical Society, and an avid poet who has published four books of poetry. Due to his writing style, one Ohio governor dubbed him "The Buckeye Poet."

Theresa Overholser is the Archivist for the Granville Historical Society and member of the Board of Managers. She enjoys researching original records as well as telling the stories of everyday people.

Larry Stevens is an Ohio Civil War bibliographer and researcher with a keen interest in the 76th Ohio Infantry and local Licking County history. He is a great grandson of Pvt. John W. Gardner.

Mark Stickle is a Ph.D. candidate in the History Department at The Ohio State University. His family has lived in Licking County since well before the Civil War.

Doug Stout is a supervisor with the Licking County Library. He inherited his passion for the Civil War from his parents. He does not remember a time that he didn't know about Lee, Grant or Gettysburg.

Martha Sturgill, originally from Massachusetts, is a retired registered nurse. She is the curator of the Alexandria Museum and cataloger and materials buyer for the Alexandria Public Library.

PREFACE

This book is a compilation of articles that appeared weekly throughout 2011 in the *Newark Advocate* newspaper to commemorate the start of the American Civil War 150 years ago and the role of Licking County in that war. The series was conceived early in 2010 during monthly meetings to coordinate county-wide events for the "Civil War 150" commemoration. The meetings were held at The Works and consisted of representatives from historical institutions, libraries, reenactors, civic groups, various media, the Licking County Convention and Visitors Bureau and other interested individuals, all very ably guided by the Managing Director of The Works, Marcia Downes.

As a result of this dynamic group, a year's worth of events were scheduled and printed in an attractive booklet by January 2011. Immediate feedback indicated that Licking County was a leader among Ohio counties in providing entertaining and educational events and opportunities about the Civil War.

Babette Wofter, Director of the Licking County Library, and Doug Stout, a supervisor there, participated in the meetings from the beginning. Due to their dedicated involvement and their confidence in me, it was suggested that I coordinate a weekly series of articles as one of the many contributions from our library. I am deeply indebted to them for the opportunity. In the process, I have learned a tremendous amount about the history of Licking County and the Civil War.

I am just as grateful for the many avid historians and writers who stepped forward to contribute to this endeavor. Without their efforts, many of the stories herein may not have been preserved for posterity. Bringing these accounts together helps to put it all into context and brings to vivid life what might have otherwise been dry history. I began to feel like I knew some of the soldiers I followed through the news, only to feel heartbroken upon reading that they were killed. But many survived and returned to take their places in business, on the farms and in families. They were all heroes, willing to give their lives for the very confusing issues behind the American Civil War.

~ *Dan Fleming*

THE UNION FOREVER!

Soldiers Wanted to fight for the Union.

THE undersigned has received authority from Columbus to recruit an Infantry Company for three year's service, or during the war. The company will have the privilege of electing its own officers, and choosing the regiment to which it will be attached. Pay ranges from $13 to $45 per month, with $100 bounty. Young men wishing to serve their country in a *good* company, voluntarily, without waiting to be drafted, should embrace this opportunity. Recruits will be received at McCune's Hardware store, in Newark, or at the office of the "Voice of the People"   J. H. PUTNAM.

Newspaper ad. From the *Newark Advocate*, August 23, 1861, p. 2.

Licking County in the Civil War:
150 Years Ago

E. Chris Evans

The commencement of the American Civil War in 1861 found the citizens of the Buckeye State not unlike their mid-western neighbors in such matters as everyday life. As divisions over slavery and secession widened, patriotism still was manifest among a majority of the populace. It is important to remember that while their "fathers brought forth on this continent" this new nation a short 85 years before, Ohio itself was a young and prideful 58. Not to be ignored, at the same time there existed a vocal minority called Peace Democrats who opposed the war and supported Southern independence. Although citizens of that persuasion could be found in every state, they were especially active in the southern half of Illinois, Indiana, and Ohio, including Licking County.

In Ohio what major industry that existed was generally in cities located on Lake Erie to the north or the Ohio River on the state's southern border. The population of the state, for the most part, was agrarian, living on small family farms or in the nearby supporting hamlets, villages and towns.

The same held true for seemingly average Licking County. In 1861, Newark with a population of 4,700 was the county seat as it still is today. If you had encountered any of the 37,000 inhabitants of the county at that time you would have found them to be ordinary, typical citizens displaying all the common conventions of civilization of the time. On the streets the young deferred to the old, people passed each other on the right, bowed recognition, lifted hats. On the Sabbath there were few who were not inclined to don their Sunday best and attend church.

Licking County, however, was anything but average. It played an important part in travel and commerce because of the Ohio and Erie Canal as well as the National Road and the Baltimore & Ohio Railroad. And in other ways, too, it exceeded the norm. It excelled in the production of corn and wheat, and with its neighboring county to the north, led the state in providing wool, all critical needs of the war effort. While Ohio as a whole provided the third greatest number of men for the armed forces, only trailing much more populous New York and Pennsylvania, Licking County did even more than its share. Drawing from a pool of some 4,880 eligible males, this county suited 3,932 of its young men (and some not so young) into uniform, slightly over 80%, bettering the state average by 10%.

Those Licking County "Boys in Blue" distinguished themselves on more than one battlefield, bringing glory to their regiments, to themselves, and to their communities back home. At the same time, the hundreds of wounds and/ or deaths to these stalwarts brought sorrow and grief to their families and loved ones. No better example of this can be found than that experienced by the Lemert family of present day Perryton, who lost four out of thirteen cousins who served, or the Henderson family of Brownsville who sacrificed to the cause three sons and a nephew.

Others were more fortunate and were able to rise to levels of acclaim. From the loins of Licking Countians came those who made names for themselves as drummer boys, men of the ranks, and generals. From the hamlet of Homer came Major General William S. Rosecrans, commander of the

Army of the Cumberland; Brownsville sired Major General Samuel Curtis, commander of the Army of the Frontier in Missouri; Granville provided Brevet Brigadier General Willard Warner who served on General Sherman's staff during the Atlanta Campaign and Major General Charles Griffin, a Corps commander in the Army of the Potomac. Griffin had the honor to be appointed by Lt. General Ulysses S. Grant to accept the surrender of General Lee's men at Appomattox Court House.

Two Newark natives completed the list of generals; Major General William Woods, who later sat as an Associate U.S. Supreme Court Justice, and his brother, West Point trained Major General Charles Woods, a division commander in Sherman's 15th Army Corps. On January 9, 1861, 1st Lieutenant Charles Woods had the honor of being the officer in command of the 200 reinforcements, along with ammunition and supplies, that President Buchanan dispatched to Ft. Sumter on board the steamship Star of the West. When the Confederates in Charleston Harbor fired on the ship forcing it to turn back to New York City, it signaled the first armed conflict against the Federal government in Washington. The ultimate result, of course, was the four year Civil War. On April 26, 1865, as the war drew to a close, this same Charles Woods, now a commander in General Sherman's army, experienced the surrender of CSA General Joseph Johnston's army in North Carolina, the largest troop surrender of the war. Thus, Licking County's Charles Woods had the distinction of being personally present at both the beginning and the ending, the Alpha and the Omega of the conflict.

Well known and recognized country-wide is the name of John L. Clem, the young 10-year-old lad who ran away from home to join the Union army. Known by the sobriquet, "The Drummer Boy of Chickamauga," Clem holds the distinction, at age 12, of being promoted to Sergeant, the youngest ever to hold the rank of NCO in the United States Army. Clem retired in 1916 as a Colonel, the last Civil War army veteran still on active duty, and following custom, was promoted one grade to the rank of Brigadier General on his last day of service. The following year, a grateful Congress promoted the retired Clem to the rank of Major General.

The many cemeteries of Licking County provide a final, serene resting place for countless veterans of that bloody Civil War. Among the graves are those of two men, who for their action in that war were recipients of their country's highest award, the Medal of Honor.

Today, Licking County is rightly known as "The Land of Legend." A good part of those legends includes not only stories concerning the families and loved ones "back home" during that fateful four-year-period, but especially the lives and heroic deeds of the officers and everyday soldiers who proudly called Licking County "home."

As you read these stories, think of your own ancestors who might have participated in one way or another. Their actions helped to shape the future of families in Licking County. This is our history.

We repeat, it is the duty of every free State to take immediate steps towards a complete organization and equipment of its militia, and to enlarge its force with special reference to the most exacting possible contingency.

– *Ohio State Journal*, Dec. 25, 1860

PRELUDE TO WAR

Cannon, Cedar Hill Cemetery, Newark, Ohio. Photo by Aaron Keirns.

Antebellum Licking County

Mark Stickle

When the nation's long-running sectional conflict erupted into full scale civil war in 1861, Licking County's formidable economic capacity was firmly harnessed to the Union cause. Half a century earlier the situation had been dramatically different. When it was organized in 1808, Licking County was an isolated and sparsely settled outpost on the country's western frontier. Area farms produced almost entirely for local consumption, and ties with the more established eastern states were shaky. Indeed, many observers predicted that the new nation would soon break apart, with the area west of the Alleghenies eventually aligning with either France or Spain.

Beginning about 1820 the situation started to change as a transportation revolution pierced the imposing Allegheny barrier. Canal boats, lake steamers, and finally railroads, provided an efficient connection between Licking County farmers and rapidly growing urban markets in the east. Market demand drew more land into cultivation, and encouraged farmers to concentrate their efforts on commodity crops. By the 1840's Ohio was the nation's undisputed agricultural powerhouse, leading the nation in the production of corn and wheat and in the raising of sheep for the wool industry. Licking County ranked fourth among the state's counties in wheat production, and solidly in the top ten in corn production. The county's sheep flock was the state's largest, and growers were well-positioned to benefit from the surge in demand associated with the manufacture of hundreds of thousands of blue woolen uniforms.

As was the case throughout the Old Northwest, the key economic unit in Licking County was the family farm. Farms were actually small family-run businesses. Although it was common to employ a hired man or surplus boys from nearby farms, the lion's share of the work was performed by the farmer, his wife and children. Labor was a chronically scarce commodity, and farm size was limited by the pool of available workers: 100 acres or so was typical, and farms in excess of 200 acres were rare. Although innovations in farm machinery certainly had an impact on productivity in the antebellum era, large-scale mechanization of most farm tasks did not come until after the Civil War.

Economic life in Licking County's villages and small towns was organized to support the agricultural economy. "Hydraulic power" was a valuable energy source, and mills were erected even on very small streams. Country stores offered access to goods which farmers could not produce for themselves, while also providing a source of credit in a society that was chronically short of currency to support even the most basic needs of exchange. A string of villages offering services to travelers dotted the National Road across the county's southern tier. The county seat at Newark was a regional hub for commodities moving on the Ohio Canal, and by the early 1850's it was acquiring importance for its location on major rail routes. Although Newark would later emerge as an important manufacturing center, the firms associated with that chapter in the area's history did not arise until the post-war era. Indeed, the war itself served as a catalyst for the industrial transformation that reshaped Licking County and Ohio in the closing decades of the nineteenth century.

Politics in 1860s Licking County

Dan Fleming

Previously, we saw a glimpse of the economic climate of Licking County just before the Civil War began. Now we will share a little of the turmoil raging on the political scene.

As in many other parts of the country, Licking County was split in its political thinking. A majority of Licking County voters in 1856 supported James Buchanan (D) in the Presidential election over John C. Fremont (R), and indeed, Buchanan won overall. By 1860, Democrats had a slight majority in Licking County by about 52%, although 52.3% of Ohio voters went with Lincoln. In the 1864 election, Lincoln won in only 7 townships out of 26 in the county (Burlington, Granville, Harrison, Hartford, Liberty, St. Albans and Washington).

The issues of abolition and states' rights were at the forefront of the discussions and arguments. Licking County Republicans had been supporting the freeing of slaves for years. Newark's first attorney and U.S. Representative (1827-1833), William Stanbery, was involved in helping an escaped slave go free during a trial in Granville, along with attorney Samuel White and Judge Samuel Bancroft. Two blacks were even permitted to vote in Granville in 1856, which created quite a stir.

For Democrats, although there might have been an underlying racist element, their stance was to support the U.S. Constitution as it was written, as well as the Fugitive Slave Law of 1850, which enforced the return of runaway slaves to their owners.

There were strong feelings on all sides, vented at political meetings throughout the county, and through the newspapers. The meetings and rallies of both parties were reported upon in their own supporting newspapers with glowing, if not exaggerated words, while political spies reported back to the opposing newspapers and manipulated the rhetoric to their own advantage. It must have been difficult for the average citizen to know what to believe. Newspapers became the trusted organs for the political parties they endorsed.

When war was declared, men of both parties lined up to enlist at the local, makeshift recruiting stations, all with the motivation of preserving the Union and bringing the seceding southern states back into it. As time went on, and especially after the Emancipation Proclamation of January 1, 1863, the issues of slavery and what to do with the freed blacks came to the forefront. Political and racial tensions grew even more, and the issues became extremely complex. The Democratic Party itself was split between those who wanted to continue the war to the bitter end (War Democrats), and those known as Peace Democrats, or Copperheads, who felt it was time to end it, even if that meant letting the southern states go their own ways.

Abolition

Dan Fleming

The subject of abolition was just as complex in Licking County as it was for the rest of the country before the American Civil War. Later in this book, we will glimpse the anti-abolition attitudes of two of her soldiers, Captain John H. Putnam and James R. Atcherly. These were typical of a great many folks in the county at the beginning of the war, who harbored fears that blacks moving up from the south would either take their jobs or become a burden upon society.

Even so, the abolition movement had been active in Licking County since at least 1834 when the first such meeting in the county was held in Granville. We see in *The History of Granville* (by Rev. Henry Bushnell, 1889) that most residents at the time favored the idea of colonization for blacks, which meant shipping them off to another country. It took a great deal of courage and conviction for abolitionists to speak out in this kind of political climate. Several prominent men were up to the challenge in the decades before the war, including Ashley A. Bancroft, Judge Samuel Bancroft, William Stanbery (Newark's first attorney), George Washington Ellis (another Newark attorney), Samuel White and William Whitney. The last two were former Denison students who had transferred to Oberlin College where they found more accepting attitudes.

In 1836 the Ohio State Anti-Slavery Convention was held in Granville. A large mob formed to oppose their procession through town by use of words, eggs, stones and fists, resulting in considerable injury and property damage. Despite that, there were several known Licking County locations on the underground railroad, including Perryton, Granville, Alexandria, Utica, Fredonia and Homer.

As a point of interest, 1836 was the same year that Newark-born Edward James Roye was teaching school in Chillicothe. His parents had settled in Newark as freed slaves. Roye travelled to Liberia in 1846 and became its President in 1870. Liberia had formed as a country from a colony that had been organized in 1822 by the American Colonization Society. It sent over 13,000 blacks there by 1867, many of whom saw this as an opportunity to gain freedom for themselves and independence from prejudice.

By the time of the Civil War, attitudes in Licking County were still split over the abolition issue. A few prominent local men who endorsed the Emancipation Proclamation included Charles B. Giffin, Isaac Smucker, Thomas J. Anderson, Major Willard Warner, and Lt. Col. William B. Woods (later promoted to Brig. General). Giffin was secretary of the Republican Central Committee and Postmaster in Newark from 1861-1866. Smucker was secretary of the Soldiers' Relief Committee and a co-founder in 1867 of the Licking County Pioneer, Historical and Antiquarian Society which was a forerunner of today's Licking County Historical Society. Anderson was a member of the Soldiers' Relief Committee and a clerk of court. Warner was a State Senator (1844-1846) and chairman of the Republican Central Committee in 1861 before his successful military career. Woods was a lawyer and member of the Ohio House from 1858 to 1862 when he joined the Union army. He was promoted to Brig. General in 1863 and took command of the 76th Ohio Volunteer Infantry regiment.

To the honorable, the General Assembly of the State of Ohio: We, your petitioners citizens of the county of Licking, and State of Ohio, do most earnestly but respectfully, petition your honorable body to enact a law which shall fully protect every inhabitant of this State in his inalienable right of Liberty, and which shall effectually abolish kidnapping and man-stealing on the soil of the State of Ohio.

– petition signed by 29 Licking County residents,
January 1863

Preparing for War

A Proclamation.

Whereas, The laws of the United States have been for some time past and now are opposed, and the execution thereof obstructed in the States of South Carolina, Georgia, Alabama, Mississippi, Louisiana and Texas, by combinations too powerful to be suppressed by the ordinary course of judicial proceedings, or by the powers vested in the Marshals by law;

Now, therefore, I, ABRAHAM LINCOLN, President of the United States, in virtue of the power in me vested by the Constitution and the laws, have thought fit to call forth, and hereby do call forth, the Militia of the several States of the Union, to the aggregate number of **75,000** in order to suppress said combinations, and to cause the laws to be duly executed. The details for this object will be immediately communicated to the State authorities through the War Department.

I appeal to all loyal citizens to favor, facilitate, and aid this effort to maintain the honor, integrity and existence of our National Union and the perpetuity of popular government, and to redress wrongs already long endured.

President Lincoln's proclamation calling for 75,000 troops. Printed in the *Newark Advocate*, April 19, 1861.

Early Recruiting

Dan Fleming

South Carolina seceded from the Union on December 20, 1860. Eight days later, the *Newark Advocate* reprinted excerpts from the *Ohio State Journal* of December 25, which stated "…it is the duty of every free State to take immediate steps towards a complete organization and equipment of its militia…" William D. Morgan, owner and editor of the *Advocate*, could not understand the reasons for this urgency, nor could he believe that U.S. citizens could be made to go to war against each other.

The *Advocate* reported on January 4, 1861 that cannon and other weapons used by Newark militia were taken from them several weeks prior and hauled to Columbus. Apparently, officials at Columbus were preparing for potential events that the ordinary citizenry could not yet imagine.

On April 12, 1861, Confederate forces opened fire on Fort Sumter in South Carolina. By then, six more states had seceded. Within a week, Ohio's Governor, William Dennison, Jr., stated his support of the Union to the Ohio General Assembly, and called for $415,000 to purchase weapons and equipment for Ohio's militias. On April 19, the *Advocate* printed President Lincoln's Proclamation calling for 75,000 volunteers from the militias of the various states, with quotas for each state. That order was handed down by the War Department through each state's governor. Ohio's first quota was 13 regiments of men between 18 and 45 years of age for a period of three months. Each regiment, including officers, would have 780 men.

Licking County did not waste any time. Leonidas Mc-Dougal (McDugall in military records), recruiting in an upstairs 3rd Street building in Newark, had his company together and on the train for Columbus by April 19. He had already been drilling a militia, most of which signed up. (It is believed he was the one who told Johnny Clem to run back home because he was too young.) McDougal became the Captain of Co. H, 3rd regiment of Ohio Volunteers.

Homer Thrall of western Licking County became the Captain of Co. B, 17th O.V.I., a 3-month unit known locally as the Granville Company. It was mustered in at Lancaster. By the end of April, Lincoln called for 40,000 more volunteers, this time for three years. Many of the men in those first three-month terms re-enlisted into 3-year companies.

The next company to form in Licking County was Co. E of the 12th O.V.I. under Capt. Andrew Legg of Newark. It was raised by June 21 and mustered in on June 28, 1861 for three years.

In July, Edwin Nichols, a Newark school teacher, raised a company that became Co. C of the 27th O.V.I., mustered in during August. Others to raise companies over that summer included Capt. D. A. B. Moore, Capt. John H. Putnam and Capt. Philip A. Crow. Putnam recruited out of McCune's Hardware in Newark, promising a salary of $13 per month for privates scaled up the ranks to $45 for 2nd Lieutenant. His Co. C, 31st regiment O.V.I. left for Camp Chase on September 13.

Camp Sherman

Doug Stout

S hall Licking County Raise a Regiment?" was the headline that Colonel Charles R. Woods ran in the October 11, 1861 *Newark Advocate*. He added, "I am authorized by the Governor to raise and take command of the 76th regiment which will go into camp at the Fair Grounds, near Newark."

This location is what we today call the Great Circle Mound on S. 21st Street. In those days it had been referred to not only as the fairgrounds, but also the old Indian fort. Neither of these names would be suitable for soldiers to call home while training, so they named it Camp Sherman. The camp was not named for William Tecumseh Sherman as we may assume. Instead, the distinction goes to his brother, John Sherman. John had served in the U.S. House of Representatives. In March of 1861, he was elected to fill the Ohio Senate seat left vacant by Salmon P Chase.

Life at Camp Sherman was no different than other camps. Days were filled with drilling and marching, teaching men to be soldiers. On Nov. 15th the *Advocate* reported that "A Thousand stand of Springfield Rifled muskets have been received at Camp Sherman for the use of the regiment. Additional supplies of clothing have also been received during the past week."

According to the annual report of the "Ohio State Board of Agriculture for 1861," measles were reported at the camp in December. Overall there were a reported 80-90 cases out of 600-700 men in the camp.

A letter from 32-year-old John Metzgar, a native of Granville who was serving with Co. B, may shed some light on a typical soldier's thoughts. The letter is dated February 6, 1862 from Camp Sherman and is written to his wife Carrie.

"Dear wife I regret very much indeed that I could not come home today to the christening but we are all in a hub-bub. Another order rumor comes today. We are not positive when we will start. We think we will go to Washington no knowing when will go. Carrie keep up your courage, I do not think we will go into service for sometime. I will not need-lessly run into danger. I hope dear Carrie that we will not be long separated ever after we move from Camp Sherman."

This time the camp rumors were true, and they marched not to Washington, but to Fort Donelson in Tennessee, and into the history books.

The camp would once more host the 76th on July 22, 1878, when 15-20,000 veterans and friends crowded the mounds to see Major General W. T. Sherman and President Hayes on a platform built over the Eagle Mound. During the program the platform collapsed, and Sherman and Hayes were only saved by leaping off. Afterwards Sherman reportedly said, "In a single afternoon one drunken carpenter nearly accomplished what 400,000 Rebels with loaded muskets failed to do in four years." Fortunately, killing a Major General and a President is not a distinction Camp Sherman has!

The Flags of The Ohio
76th Volunteer Infantry: "Newark's Own"

E. Chris Evans

Each regiment of the U.S. Army has a stand of colors, or battle flags as some refer to them. This stand consists of two flags: a national flag and a regimental flag (blue if infantry, red if artillery, yellow if cavalry). During the Civil War it was quite popular, almost customary, for the ladies of the regiment's town to provide and present these "colors" to the regiment. The same holds true for "Newark's Own," the 76th Ohio Volunteer Infantry Regiment.

As the mustering date into Federal service of February 7, 1862 approached, the members of the Ladies Soldiers' Aid Society decided upon a plan to raise the needed money to obtain such a Stand of Colors. A Military Festival and Fair was held at City Hall on January 27th. This extra successful event consisted of an "elegant" dinner followed by the expected oratorical presentations and "music and dancing sufficiently good to retain a crowded hall till four o'clock in the morning," according to a report in the *Advocate* of January 31, 1862. With the proceeds of this event the ladies were able to settle their debts from providing "housewife" sewing kits and extra stockings to the men who had earlier entered service in other local units, and to purchase the colors for the 76th.

No doubt working long hours, perhaps into the night, the Society's members rushed to finish the embroidery of a large eagle on the regimental flag as well as painting on it an unfurled ribbon with the unit's designation, *76th Regiment OV,*

Larry Stevens standing next to the regimental flag of the 76th Ohio Volunteer Infantry. From the collection of Larry Stevens.

USA. These flags were used during battle as a focal point for the men to rally around, as audible signals could not be heard over the din; thus their importance. At the same time, they become a target for the enemy, either to kill or wound the flag bearer, or if possible, to capture the colors themselves.

In any event, the colors were not completed when the regiment left by train for Cincinnati on Sunday, February 9th. As Major Charles Dana Miller of the 76th later wrote, "Here (Cincinnati) we marched up Front Street to the (river) landing and went aboard two steamboats, the *Universe* and the *Diamond.* The regimental colors were presented and unfurled to the breeze for the first time on the steamer deck as the boats shoved off from the shore" on their way to the battle of Ft. Donelson, Tennessee.

This stand of colors was carried through all the major battles of the western theater including Mission Ridge, but the regimental flag was captured at Ringgold Gap in Georgia by Rebel "Johnnies" on November 27, 1863. A second set of colors was presented at Bridgeport, Alabama on May 4, 1864. As Major Miller wrote: "The Regiment received its new stand of colors, which were brought from Ohio by Colonel Warner to replace our first flags, so tattered and torn in service that they could hardly be unfurled with safety." At a Grand Army of the Republic (G.A.R) reunion in Newark on September 20, 1916, members of the Confederate 1st Arkansas returned the flag of the 76th which they had held over 50 years. Today the flags of "Newark's Own," the 76th O.V.I., are at the Ohio Historical Society in Columbus.

FLAG CAPTURED DURING CIVIL WAR RETURNED TO YANKEE COLOR BEARER

W. C. Montgomery of Company D, 76th Ohio, receiving tattered emblem, more than 50 years old, from Mrs. Townes R. Legh, matron of honor at the Jacksonville (Fla.) Confederate Veterans' reunion. At her left is Colonel Kibler, one of the few remaining "boys in gray."

W. C. Montgomery of Company D, 76th O.V.I. receives their battle flag back from the 1st Arkansas.

MOVING OUT

Temptations of the Camp.

These words will not reach many who have volunteered to fight for their country, but it will reach some, and more, perhaps, of those who will do so at some early future time. It would be a sad result of this war, and a great misfortune, if those who have so nobly stepped forward for their country's defense should, after having fought their battles, return to their homes polluted in morals, addicted to liquor, broken down in health by vicious practices, and unfitted to resume the peaceful avocations of life. Removed from home, and the restraints of society of women, with many idle hours to be passed in some way, with monotony to be broken up by all practicable measures, and with a constant desire for excitement, it will be very hard for young men to resist temptation to vicious indulgences in the various ways in which they present themselves to the soldiers. Now it should be the definite aim and determination of every man who enlists in this war to bring his mind and body out of it unpolluted—to return to his home at last, if he is permitted to do so, as good, as pure and as healthy as when he left it.—

Newspaper editorial. In the *Newark Advocate*, June 7, 1861.

A Traveling Library for the Troops

Dan Fleming

Leonidas McDougal (McDugall in the military rosters) of Newark was Captain of Company H of the Newark Militia, the first 3-month company to be raised in Licking County to serve during the American Civil War. The company was later moved into the 3rd Ohio Volunteer Infantry regiment under Colonel Isaac H. Marrow. The 3rd regiment was blessed with the services of Chaplain Erastus A. Strong.

Rev. Strong was born in New York in 1809 and married a woman from Connecticut in 1833. She died in 1840, and he remarried in 1844. At some point he was ordained as a minister in Columbus, Ohio. He enlisted with the 3rd regiment as its chaplain in June 1861.

Already by that date, people back home were concerned that their young men were learning bad habits in the ranks, in the forms of profanity, obscenity, indolence, gambling and whiskey. Rev. Strong saw a need to keep the morality of the troops elevated as well as handling their spiritual needs. He devised a plan to keep their minds working in positive ways and to help educate them for vocational or higher endeavors once they returned home.

Rev. Strong established a library to travel with the regiment. We do not know how many books it contained, or the titles, but it was not to exceed 500 pounds in weight. More importantly, the books were not just of a religious nature. They were signed out to the troops, just as in a public library. Rev. Strong did not stop there. He enlisted 20 men from among the officers and troops to volunteer to teach such things as business, ancient and modern languages and higher mathematics to the others.

Unfortunately for Capt. McDougal, he did not live long enough to benefit from this special education. He was killed at the Battle of Perryville, Kentucky on October 8, 1862. Other Newark boys were wounded during a raid from northern Alabama into Georgia in 1863. The library was probably long gone before that, because the regiment had participated in several battles by then.

The entire company was captured near Rome, Georgia in April 1863. Rev. Strong was held in Atlanta and at Libby Prison in Virginia, but the company was paroled and sent back to Camp Chase at Columbus, Ohio. This parole was a kind of honor system, relying on their word that they would not rejoin the war until an exchange took place. This practice became too cumbersome and was ended about halfway through the war.

Finally, after their three years of service were completed, Company H was mustered out in June 1864, and the soldiers straggled home. Rev. Strong suffered ill health and died in 1866. He was buried at Gambier, Ohio.

Typical Meals of the Soldiers

Anne Kennedy

Think of the meal you just had. If it was well-balanced, you probably had some protein, dairy, vegetables, fruit and grains. A Civil War soldier, though, might eat a weevil-filled piece of hardtack, ground into pieces with the butt of his rifle and fried in bacon grease to make it taste slightly better. Did you have a cup of coffee this morning? Our Civil War soldier probably had one, too. Most soldiers roasted their coffee beans in the fire, smashed them into pieces with the butt of their rifles, boiled them in whatever water they found, and strained the liquid through a piece of fabric.

A Union soldier's daily ration was supposed to be 3/4 pounds of pork or bacon, or 1 1/4 pounds of fresh or salt beef, plus 18 ounces of flour or bread, or 12 ounces of hardtack, or 1 1/4 pounds of cornmeal. Each 100-man company was given 8 quarts of peas or beans (about 15 pounds), or 10 pounds of rice; 6-10 pounds of coffee or 1 1/2 pounds of tea; 12-15 pounds of sugar; 4 quarts of vinegar; 2 quarts of salt; 4 ounces of pepper; 1/2 bushel of potatoes; and 1 quart of molasses.

In theory, the Confederate troops had similar rations as Union soldiers. In reality, the South's low supplies and lack of adequate transportation meant its soldiers constantly dealt with food shortages. Cornmeal and bacon were more available than flour and salt beef. Like the Union, Confederate soldiers would fry everything in bacon grease to improve the taste. Coffee was in such short supply that soldiers would roast anything from peanuts to acorns. One thing the southern soldiers were not short of was tobacco. Sometimes, during a lull in fighting, Confederates would trade Union soldiers tobacco for coffee.

Soldiers from Licking County eagerly awaited packages from the Soldiers' Aid Society. The packages were a welcome break from the normally bland diets. The ladies from Newark sent many kinds of food to the front including canned and dried fruits, vegetables, cordials, tinned meat, candy, cakes, bottles of wine and much more. These supplies were carefully packed and sent directly to the soldiers at the front or to the Sanitary Commission, which distributed supplies to the sick. The soldiers frequently sent thank you notes to the Soldiers' Aid Society which were published in the newspaper. Charles Pierce, the surgeon of the 76th, told the ladies, "The supplies are in excellent condition, and are most acceptable, while their real value is enhanced by the remembrance that they are the gift of kind friends *at home*."

Hardtack Recipe
(modified for modern kitchens)

Mix 5 cups of flour to 1 cup of water containing 1/2 teaspoon of salt.

Knead into a dough, and roll out to a 3/8-inch thickness.

Cut into approximately 3-inch squares, and pierce each with a fork or ice pick several times.

Bake in a 400 degree oven for 30 minutes or until slightly brown.

Unhappy Letter from James R. Atcherly

Dan Fleming

The early letters home from James R. Atcherly of Capt. John H. Putnam's Company H, 31st Regiment, painted a rosy picture of camp life and marches. It was different, however, on June 2, 1862, four miles south of Corinth, Mississippi. He said, "I write to you, if not from the depths of my heart, at least from the depths of a wilderness. Wilderness. Ugh, that doesn't imply half the horrors of this wretched, deserted, god-forsaken, 'skeeter-inhabited region. From the time we reached Pittsburg Landing [Tennessee] up to the present, which is a little more than six weeks, we have never been out of the woods. Nothing but woods, woods, and bugs, bugs, continually and eternally. Did you ever see a wood tick?...They have picked me clean; and everyone knows that I could but ill spare it... so that I now go by the delightful cognomen of 'Bones,' Spindle,' or 'Shanks.' But then there's one consolation, even for me. I don't have so much to carry, and that's quite a consideration when you remember that we have a knapsack, sixty rounds of ammunition, canteen and haversack to carry."

Then he complained that, after weeks of labor in preparation for a siege of Corinth, the rebels "had given us the slip and gone, baggage, guns and all...without saying good bye."

Atcherly then vented his political views. "The conviction is gradually forcing itself upon us that as soon as we can dispose of the rebels, that is, bring them back once more beneath the old flag, there will be one more task for us to perform...to march, Cromwell like, upon Washington, and purge both Houses of the traitors or idiots (I hardly know which to call them) who now disgrace the seats where once great men sat..."

He went on to say, "The fact is, you can't imagine how mortifying and discouraging it is to think that while we are exerting ourselves to the utmost, suffering all the horrors which a tropical climate imposes, to advance our cause and preserve our country, a large party at the North who claim to love the same banner and country for which we are fighting, seem to be doing all they can to hold us back." He was referring to abolitionists. The temperament and motivation of many Licking Countians at the time, including some of the early volunteers, was to preserve the union and bring the secessionist states back into it. Slavery was not yet the issue at this early stage of the war. Atcherly says, "Let us first save ourselves and the country...and settle this [slavery] question afterwards."

Atcherly volunteered to serve with Capt. Putnam in January 1862. He had been a member of the prestigious Young Men's Forum in Newark, which lost most of its members to the early volunteer effort, including two commissioned officers, nine non-commissioned officers, and nine privates. Only three regular members stayed behind as of January 1862. In August that year, Atcherly returned home to recruit more troops for Putnam. After his tour of duty, he came back and entered into business with Putnam in April 1863 selling hats, caps, boots, shoes and hosiery on the south side of the Square.

Capt. D. A. B. Moore's Squabble with the Quartermaster

Dan Fleming

In a letter home, printed in the *Advocate* on January 31, 1862, Captain D. A. B. Moore of Company D, 1st Cavalry, wrote eloquently of his disagreements with Quartermaster James M. Allen during a long march in Kentucky from Camp Buell to about five miles outside Louisville. It sprinkled in the morning and became a downpour by 11:00 a.m. At 5:00 they marched another 21 miles and pitched their tents. This is when they discovered that Allen had failed to obtain rations for the men and forage for the horses. So Moore went to a local farmer, a Union man, and purchased seven large hams, plus enough oats at a discount for the horses.

Reveille sounded at 4:00 a.m. and they were on the march by 6:00, wading through a foot of water due to a dike break upstream. They managed to travel 25 miles non-stop through an all-day rain. Quartermaster Allen ordered them to pitch their tents near a creek. Some did, but Moore refused, setting up near a hill instead. Allen told Moore to consider himself under arrest for disobeying orders. Moore "told him to go to a warmer climate." Only three companies did as they were told by camping near the creek.

They slept in wet blankets. Around 9:00 p.m. a terrible rain storm came up with thunder and lightning for about an hour. Their comrades near the creek began screaming. The stream had swollen and swept everything away—tents, saddles, blankets and supplies. Next morning, they waded knee-deep in a flood to recover what they could, while their horses were tied and standing over their knees in water.

The captains got together and agreed that they would not proceed any farther if the Quartermaster was to choose their campsites. They protested to their regiment commander, Lt. Col. Smith, who agreed with them and assigned someone else to that duty.

Meanwhile, Quartermaster Allen approached Moore and told him he was released from arrest. Moore said that he never considered himself under arrest in the first place, and that if Allen did not go take care of real business he would make him go into the water and look for their things. That unfortunate gentleman left camp and resigned his post on January 28.

They marched 17 miles that day, leaving behind half of each of the three companies who had lost their goods to continue looking for them. They estimated that $5,000 would not replace all that they lost.

Ohio Squirrel Hunters in the Civil War

Elizabeth Bicking

By the summer of 1862 the Civil War action was just across the Ohio River from the Queen City, Cincinnati. The Union Army had been defeated in Richmond, Kentucky. Confederate General Kirby Smith was planning to repeat his success in Cincinnati and perhaps beyond into the State of Ohio. With this threat, Ohio's Governor Tod on August 30, 1862 officially announced:

"Our southern border is threatened with invasion. I have therefore to recommend that all the loyal men of our counties at once form themselves into military companies and regiments to beat back the enemy at any and all points he may attempt to invade our state. Gather up all the arms in the country and furnish yourselves with ammunition for the same. The service will be of but a few days' duration. The soil of Ohio must not be invaded by the enemies of our glorious government."

By September 5, over 15,000 men from 65 Ohio counties had arrived in Cincinnati, mostly by rail. There were 404 from Licking County, young and old from all backgrounds, and most with no military training. They wore their own clothing and took their own hunting rifles and ammunition. A confederate scout was said to have commented, "They call them 'Squirrel Hunters,' farm boys that never had to shoot at the same squirrel twice."

The Squirrel Hunters helped dig trenches and other fortifications, but saw no real action against the enemy, who soon retreated. Governor Tod wired Secretary of War, Edwin M.

Stanton, on September 13:

"The minute-men of Squirrel Hunters responded gloriously to the call for the defense of Cincinnati. Thousands reached the city, and thousands more were en route for it. The enemy having retreated all have been ordered back. This uprising of the people is the cause of the retreat. You should acknowledge publicly this gallant conduct. Please order Quarter-master Burr to pay all transportation bills, upon my approval."

With that, the minute-men of Ohio, the Squirrel Hunters, were discharged. Certificates were printed for them, many of which may be found today. In 1911, the Ohio legislature finally approved to pay those who yet survived for their services, but only a few were actually paid after a long verification process. They received $13.

Editor's Note

After the foregoing article was printed in the *Advocate*, the following account turned up which illustrates the spirit out in the country. It was written by Mary Ellen Lemert Montgomery, sister of Thaddeus Lemert who had organized Company A of the 76th Ohio Volunteer Infantry. She was also wife of Henry A. Montgomery who answered the call for "squirrel hunters."

"On May 3, 1864, Henry was called to enter the army and was classified as the Muskingum Home Guards to serve a hundred days...He and my brother Thomas had also answered the call for farmers and citizens to defend Cincinnati from a large force from the South. They were called 'The Squirrel Hunters Brigade' for they took their own guns, the ones they were accustomed to use when hunting. When the danger to Cincinnati was over, these farmers and citizens were honorably discharged by Governor Tod of Ohio. This was in 1862."

And this, from a letter from Mary Ellen to her son, Edward Montgomery :

"In September after you were three years old, your Pa was called out to defend Cincinnati from the rebels, in what was called the Squirrel Hunters' Call. We had a very large crop of peaches that year. We were up in the peach orchard at work drying peaches, when the two church bells commenced ringing and kept it up until all the people within sound of it went to town and found out what was wanted.

Pa came back and said he was going—would start from Newark at 12 o'clock. So I boiled a ham and made a haversack and Grandma molded bullets, while Pa cleaned up the old musket. We kiln-dried about six bushels of peaches and sent about half of them to the 76th Regiment, where there were a great many sick soldiers."

The Squirrel Hunter's Discharge.

Our Southern Border was menaced by the enemies of our Union. David Tod, Governor of Ohio called on the Minute Men of the State and the Squirrel Hunters came by thousands to their rescue. You *Loammi Inscho* were one of them and this is your Honorable Discharge.

September 1862.

Approved by
DAVID TOD, Governor

Cha¹ W. Hill
Adjt. Gen. of Ohio

Malcolm McDowell
Major & A.D.C.

State of Ohio
Department of Auditor of State

Columbus, Ohio, MAY 28 1912 191

Mr. Loammi Inscho,

Vareita, Ohio.

Dear Sir:

Please find enclosed Warrant No. 16740, on the Treasurer of the State, payable to your order for $ 13.90, being amount due you from

Squirrel Hunter Service

I have the honor to be,

Yours very truly,

A. V. Donahey,
Auditor of State

By _____ Chief Clerk

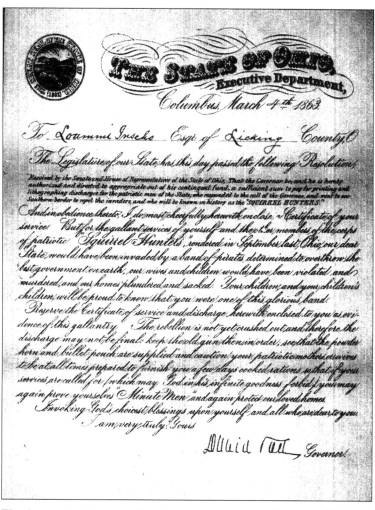

The documents shown on these two pages are a complete set of Squirrel Hunter certificates issued to Laomi Inscho, brother of Leonidas Inscho. Copied with permission from the collection of E. Chris Evans, gifted to him by Inscho's descendants.

Abstracted from an article of the same name in *Licking Lantern* (newsletter of the Licking County Genealogical Society), Vol. 36, No. 2, 2011.

The Battle of North Mountain Depot, West Virginia

Doug Stout

July 3,1864: the men of the 135th O.V.I., companies B and F probably wondered what they had gotten themselves into.

They had started out in Licking County as the 5th Ohio National Guard. They combined with the 32nd Battalion National Guard from Hardin County to form the 135th O.V.I., to serve a 100 day enlistment. They were sworn in at Camp Chase on May 11, 1864 and immediately were sent to Cumberland, Maryland to meet the Confederate threat. Jubal Early and a force of 14,000 troops were marching up the Shenandoah Valley, according to a plan laid out by General Lee. Lee and his army were bottled up by General Grant at Petersburg, Virginia, and it was Lee's hope that Early could open up another front in the war to divert Union forces from Petersburg so Lee could break the siege.

The 135th had been ordered from Maryland to the area of Martinsburg, West Virginia where they were to guard the B&O Railroad. On May 8th the 135th was distributed along the railroad, and Companies B and F were sent to North Mountain Depot. There they found a 25x25 two-story blockhouse surrounded by a ditch and abatis. They numbered just under 200 men and were under the command of Captain Ulysses S. Westbrook of Gratiot, Ohio.

As the Rebels approached Martinsburg, orders were sent all along the B&O line to fall back, but since the telegraph wires had been cut the men at North Mountain never received the orders. On the morning of July 3 they awoke to find the skirmish line of General John McCausland advancing. There are discrepancies as to how many rebels there were. Sources say anywhere from 1,000-3,000, but it seemed to the 135th like the whole Confederate army was attacking them. The rebel advance displayed a white flag of truce, but Captain Westbrook ordered it fired upon. The blockhouse offered some protection, being of pine logs with firing holes, so the rifles carried by McCausland's men could not penetrate the logs. Artillery was brought up slowly, for the 135th was laying a deadly fire down upon the cannoneers, but once in place the first shot shattered logs and set the roof on fire. More shells were leveled at the blockhouse, and by noon after five hours of fighting the 135th surrendered. There were many wounded, but only one killed. Though these men were not hardened veterans they had offered up quite a resistance. According to Private Thomas Hayes of company B, it was the consensus of the men that if Captain Westbrook had been a sober man when they were attacked, they would not have been captured!

Most were sent to Andersonville Prison in Georgia, where many would die of starvation and disease. Reports vary, but only 60-65 men would ever live to see their homes again. At least 70 of those who died in prison were from Licking County; 54 at Andersonville, 10 at Florence, S.C. and a few at other locations.

After the war, Captain Westbrook made a request to General McCausland that he return his sword for a family relic, as "he had buckled on his sabre and he has had it a longer time than I had." There is no record if Capt. Westbrook's request was ever granted.

WOMEN BACK HOME

Detail of a photograph of a group of women from Newark, Ohio who gave aid to soldiers in hospitals during the Civil War.
From the collection of Aaron Keirns.

Fashion & Fuss...
Women's Clothing of the Civil War Era

Linda A. Leffel

Today's fashions can be high-style and exclusive, but most average Americans are a very casual society—often way too casual if you ask me, as one who remembers going to the downtown Columbus Lazarus with my mother, wearing a fancy dress, with little white gloves to shop and then eat in the Chintz Room! I imagine ladies of the mid-1800s would be appalled at some outfits worn today—but yet, might be envious of the more simple apparel when thinking of the constricting attire most in their era wore. Recently, Mary Ann Bina, area historical-fashion enthusiast, and I sat down and discussed fashions of this era, and the impact the war had on the dress of the day.

Coming into the Civil War era, women were still dressing in Victorian prim-and-proper style, with the elite of the north and plantation belles of the south wearing a range of specialized clothing for all occasions. Although there were always working-class women and poor who had jobs outside the home, most women did not. The proper outfit for the right occasion was of utmost importance for many. The wealthy might wear several dresses each day, while working-class women only owned two or three everyday dresses, plus a "Sunday-best" outfit. Typical ladies of the time wore layers upon layers of clothing, which was not only restricting, but also very time-consuming to assemble (think of Scarlet in *Gone with the Wind* holding the bedpost as she is tied into her corset). Usual layers might consist first of drawers (loose underpants), a chemise (long undershirt), and stockings with garters; secondly, a corset with "stays" of whale bone, a crinoline, hoop skirt, and layers of petticoats, followed by a petticoat bodice and cover for the corset, or a camisole; thirdly, a bodice, outer skirt (possibly with suspenders), and a belt; and last, slippers or shoes of satin, velvet, or knit. If leaving the house, you'd need to include a shawl or jacket, gloves, button-up boots, hat, purse—and you wouldn't want to forget your handkerchief, fan, or even a pocket watch! Such styles were not only impractical, but dangerous, as wide-sweeping dresses could easily catch on fire!

The Civil War was a turning point for women's attire as roles for many women changed. With men gone to war, women were responsible for new duties, which necessitated being less constricted. During the war, material available for clothing was sparse (again, think of GWTW's Scarlet with clothing made from draperies). Popularity of the sewing machine after the war led to more women becoming dress makers, and offering a greater variety of styles. There were two Newark dressmakers listed in the 1860s directories: Miss M.B. Smith on the Public Square, and Miss M. M. Van Atta on Main and Canal Streets.

Note: This story served as a promotion for a program on March 12, 2011 called "Fashion and Fuss" at the Buckingham House, presented by Mary Ann Bina and hosted by the Licking County Historical Society. She shared a collection of period clothing and accessories.

Quilting; a Piece of Our History

Martha Sturgill

All generations of American women have used their skills to create a warm environment for their families, friends and neighbors, from cooking a meal to piecing a patchwork coverlet. Gifts of food and needlework have been part of the American tradition of hospitality from earliest times. A new neighbor, a new baby or any natural disaster, were opportunities for this expression to shine.

The block-type quilting that we know today had its beginnings after 1840 when textile manufacture made patterned cotton cloth affordable and readily available. No longer did spinning and weaving have to precede all construction of useful or artistic textile objects. With the ease of obtaining a wide variety of fabrics came an expansion of the housewife's horizons.

Before the Civil War, quilts were made and sold at fairs along with other needlework crafts with the proceeds supporting social causes such as abolition. Anti-slavery poetry and sayings were added to the items to help raise awareness of the plight of the slave. The first Anti-Slavery Fair was held in Boston in 1834 and was so successful that the idea spread from New England to Pennsylvania and Ohio.

After April 1861 when the war began, the quilting tradition took on a new importance as husbands, sons and fathers went off to war. Women on both sides were active in making quilts to raise funds for patriotic causes and soldiers' relief. In the South women used fancy silks and satins to make elaborate quilts, which were sold to pay for the iron-clad gun

Pre-Civil War Pioneer Album Quilt from the collection of Liz Bicking.
The pattern is called Christian Cross, Chimney Sweep or Pioneer Friendship
Album, which often contained signatures of friends in the center. Sashing to
set off the blocks came into use around 1840. This pattern was most popular
in the 1840s and 1850s. This quilt was given to Florence Luckhurst of New
Haven, CT by Douglas Abrams in the mid-1970s. Doug believed it was made
by his grandmother on his mother's side, Mrs. Smith Weed Tryon of Darian, CT
(Noraton, CT). Douglas' mother Micina Merrit Crabb gave the quilt to Elizabeth
L. Bicking in the 1980s.

boats needed by the Confederacy. As naval battles were lost
and fabric became more scarce in the South, women turned
their efforts to making serviceable coverlets for the soldiers
themselves or to purchase much-needed medical supplies.

In the North the fairs continued, but the proceeds went
to war-related causes. It became the job of the United States
Sanitary Commission to collect and distribute the 4-by-7-
foot quilts needed for the servicemen. An estimated 250,000
quilts and comforters were made for Union soldiers during
the four-year course of the war. Very few have survived for
two reasons; they were either worn out or soldiers were buried in them.

Front side of a Civil War theme quilt made in 2004 by Cristina Matheny Carr of Johnstown, Ohio (now of Stonybrook, Long Island, NY). It was given to her nephew, Steven Hicks for his graduation from Northridge High School. It is all hand-pieced, appliqued and quilted. Cristina has made 60-70 quilts since high school. This one won first place at the Hartford Fair in 2007.

Back side of the Civil War quilt shown at top. This side contains a key to each block and its significance, surrounding a large central appliquéd crest with stylized flowers. The borders have appliquéd flowers with flags in the four corners.

During the war, album quilts and flag quilts were especially popular. Quilt blocks with names like *Underground Railroad*, *Log Cabin*, *Lincoln's Platform* and *Sherman's March* became popular after the war. Patterns for blocks were passed down by way of sketches in a letter or by sample blocks pasted together quickly and kept in a stack to refer to later. Quilting patterns did not become somewhat standardized until the advent of ladies' magazines such as *Godey's Ladies' Book*. By the late 1800s farm magazines and pattern companies were printing and naming traditional blocks for the use of quilters, but regional names still persist, causing confusion when writing about quilting.

Note: This story served as a promotion for a program called "Quilting from the Civil War to the Present" at the Alexandria Public Library and the Alexandria Museum from April 2 to May 1, 2011, where historic and modern quilts were on display by local owners. The quilts dated back to the 1850s.

Socks for Soldiers

Anne Kennedy

During the American Civil War, Soldiers' Aid Societies sent food, clothing, bandages, money, and much more to soldiers at the front and to those recovering in hospitals. The Newark Soldiers' Aid Society regularly published records of their donations in the *Newark Advocate*. Some of the most common donations were pairs of handknitted socks.

Prior to the war, store-bought socks were simply not available. On average, a knitter would produce between 7 and 10 pairs for her family each year. Once war was declared, the constant need for new socks and shoes was great. Knitters began doubling or tripling their normal production. Accomplished knitters could make three pairs per week!

The differences between modern and Civil War knitting are great. Then, most people learned from family members and friends. Today, much knitting information is shared online at sites like Ravelry.com or published in books and magazines.

Modern patterns carefully explain what size of yarn and needles should be used in order to get the correct number of stitches per inch or gague. Also, needle diameters are standardized. During the 1860s, however, needle and yarn sizes varied widely. Some patterns would instruct the knitter to "use the usual size" needles and others would list needle sizes which were only sold by the publisher of the pattern. Additionally, 1860s patterns assumed that the knitter would already have much prior knowledge. This sock pattern or "receipt" came from an 1861 issue of *Scientific American*:

"The following rules are laid down for the direction of ladies wishing to knit socks for the soldiers:—Get large needles and a coarse yarn; cast on seventy-eight stitches, and knit the leg ten inches before setting the heel. The heel should be three and a half inches long, and knit of double yarn, one fine and one coarse, for extra strength. The foot should be eleven or twelve inches long."

As you can see, the pattern relies much on the knitter's experience. Many modern sock patterns explain in detail which technique you should use for each part of the sock.

Most of today's knitters would never dream of making a sock with such fine yarn and needles as a Civil War knitter. Sock knitters in the 1860s used very fine needles or "pins" which correspond to modern U.S. needle sizes 00 to 00000. A U.S. 00 has a diameter of 1.75 mm and a U.S. 00000 is 1 mm. The gauge for Civil War socks could be anywhere from 8 to 15 stitches per inch or higher. The fine yarn used corresponds with today's laceweight or finer yarn. Modern handknit socks usually have a gauge of 6 to 8 stitches per inch and are made with U.S. 1 needles which are 2.5 mm in diameter.

If you would like more information about historical knitting, consider these works: *No Idle Hands: The Social History of American Knitting* by Anne Mcdonald, *A History of Hand Knitting* by Richard Rutt, *Knitting America* by Susan Strawn, and *Piecework* magazine, March/April 2009.

Soldiers' Aid Society

Dan Fleming

On October 11, 1861, an anonymous notice appeared in the *Newark Advocate*, asking all ladies of Newark to meet the next day at City Hall to organize and operate a Soldiers' Aid Society. It "will do much service in relieving the wants and sufferings of the neighbors and friends who go from among us to serve their country on the battle field." On the same page was a notice from M. C. Meigs, Quartermaster-General of the United States, asking families to donate blankets for the troops. The Soldiers' Aid Society would fill that request and much more.

Officers were elected at the first meeting, resulting in Mrs. Israel Dille being President, and Amelia K. Wing being Secretary and Treasurer. Twelve weeks later, the group reported on its activities. Already by November 5, it had sent a box of socks, mittens, gloves, shirts, drawers and blankets to Capt. McDougal's company. On November 23 it sent 75 straw ticks to the companies of Capt. Kibler and Capt. Coman, both of the 76th Regiment. More clothing was sent to Capt. Legg's company on November 28, and to Capt. Wehrle's company on December 20.

Over the next two years, the Society also sent supplies to Lt. Col. William B. Woods, Gen. G. B. Wright, the companies of Captains Nichols, Putnam and Crow, as well as Camp Sherman, the Columbus Soldiers' Aid Society, the hospital at Nashville, and the O.S. Relief Association in Washington, D. C.

The Society stated that it would "remain in existence so

long as it can be of any assistance to Licking County soldiers, or to the poor of Newark and so long as the ladies of Newark weary not in well-doing." It not only sent supplies directly to the field, but it also sent hospital supplies to the Cincinnati Sanitary Commission to be distributed to various hospitals. Back home, the Society even donated needed coal, clothing and food to the poor.

By early 1863, items sent to the field besides clothing and bandages included canned and dried fruits of all kinds, vegetables, catsup, jam and jelly, brandy peaches, tobacco, and lots of wine. The food and some clothing were donated by families, while fundraisers were held to pay for other items. These included a Continental Supper in May 1862, a Continental Tea Party and a Firemen's Union Ball in June 1862, and an entertainment program in January 1863.

There were no further notices in the *Advocate* about the Society's activities after April 1863, until Mrs. Lucius Case became its President in June 1864. Her husband was a Newark attorney and one of the framers of the 1851 Ohio Constitution. Lucius died at home on July 24 that year, and notices about the Society completely stopped. The torch was taken up by a new group called the Young Ladies Soldiers' Aid Society of Granville, which sent its first shipment of hospital supplies on August 24, 1864. This group held a fundraising festival in November that year, which was called the most successful one of its kind in the county, raising $500.

There will be a Festival for the benefit of "Soldiers' Aid Society," in the Town Hall, Granville, on Friday evening, November Sixth, 1863. A dinner for the old people will be given at the Hall, at two o'clock P.M. of same day. Admission 25 cts. "Come one, come all."

– Newark Advocate, Oct. 30, 1863

MEANWHILE

Daniel Decatur Emmett. From the book, *Daniel Decatur Emmett, Author of 'Dixie'* by Charles Burleigh Galbreath (1904).

I Wish I Was in Dixie Land

James P. Lukens

With all the interest in the American Civil War this year, I am reminded of a story by Civil War historian, Webb Garrison, about how unique a role the song *Dixie* played for North and South, friend and foe at the dawning of the war. According to Garrison, both sides were very fond of the song from the beginning. We have Mt. Vernon, Ohio native, Daniel Decatur Emmett, to thank for composing this still popular melody.

After a short stint in the army (he lied about his age) as a fifer and drummer, Emmett, a self- taught musician, joined the circus as a blackface banjoist and singer. By 1843, he was part of a minstrel troupe, performing and writing songs, even going to England, and playing for standing room only crowds. Later he became a member of Bryant's Minstrels, one of the most popular blackface minstrel groups of the time. It was while he was with the Bryants that Emmett composed *Dixie*.

"No use to write a song unless it will catch on enough to be sung in the streets," Emmett thought. "Suddenly, I jumped up and sat down at my table to work. For the first time I had an idea and in less than an hour I had the first verse and chorus," he reported. "After that it was easy. I sang it to my wife. It was all finished except a name and she didn't hesitate." "Why, call it *I Wish I Was in Dixie Land*," and the song was on its way.

Dixie was first sung on April 4, 1859 and was an instant sensation. It was used by other minstrel shows, and its lyrics were often printed in newspapers. Since abolitionists and slave-owners alike frequented the blackface minstrel shows in New York, Philadelphia, Washington and Richmond, they were all soon familiar with the rousing tune. It was first performed in the South in Charleston, South Carolina in December 1860. About three months later, it was used in a production of *Pocahontas* in New Orleans, which brought seven encores.

The song was so popular that different groups began setting their own lyrics to the melody, which was quite surprising to Emmett. "I couldn't believe it when I heard the version that came out of the Republican convention," he said. Then on February 18, 1861, *Dixie* was used at the inauguration of Jefferson Davis as President of the Confederate States of America. It was not long after this that it became the informal national anthem for the South.

Meanwhile, by the end of 1861, many in the North also claimed the song for themselves, where it was in wide use until at least the siege of Vicksburg, Mississippi in 1863.

Adapted by permission from article, "North and South Embrace 'Dixie" in the *Licking County Historical Society Quarterly*, Autumn 2011 by James P. Lukens.

Dealing With Spies

Dan Fleming

I have often wondered how easy it might have been to be a spy during the Civil War for either side, especially for anyone who could conceal their local accent or dialect. There were spies throughout the war, both men and women, North and South. As the war dragged on, however, it became more and more difficult to engage in such a practice.

In late 1864, a Confederate spy was even caught in Newark at the train station. Sam B. Davis had been a prison guard at Andersonville Prison before taking an assignment to travel to Canada in disguise and with a British passport. Confederate spies frequently met in safety in Canada to hatch their plots.

As Davis returned by train through Columbus, Ohio, two former Union prisoners who had been exchanged recognized him and discretely had the conductor telegraph ahead to the provost marshal at Newark. Davis was picked up at the depot and put into the Newark jail. He went to trial in Cincinnati in January 1865, was sent to Johnson's Island in Lake Erie, and sentenced to hang on February 17, 1865. On the appointed morning of the hanging, word came that President Lincoln himself had commuted the sentence after pleadings from Davis' family. Davis then spent months at Fort Warren in Boston until long after the war ended. Eventually some former Union prisoners from Andersonville protested his treatment and secured his release.

Davis had faced his hanging bravely, knowing the risk from the start. On July 23, 1862, Union Major General Pope had issued his General Order No. 11 to deal with potential spies:

"Commanders of army corps, divisions, brigades and detached commands, will proceed immediately to arrest all disloyal male and female citizens within their lines, or within their reach, or within their respective stations. Such as are willing to take the oath of allegiance to the United States, and will furnish sufficient security for its observance, shall be permitted to remain at home and pursue, in good faith their accustomed avocations. Those who refuse shall be conducted to or beyond the extreme pickets of this army, and be notified if found again anywhere within our lines, or at any point in our rear, they will be considered as spies, and subjected to the extreme vigor of military law. If any person, having taken the oath of allegiance as above specified, shall be found to have violated it, he shall be shot, and his property seized and applied to the public use.

"All communication with any person whatever, living within the lines of the enemy, is positively prohibited, except through the military authorities, and in the manner specified by military law; and any person concerned in writing, or carrying messages, will be considered and treated as a spy within the limits of the United States army."

This would have made it especially difficult for families and friends who were divided between both sides. It would also not have been wise to be a war protester in those years.

Gifts to Newspapers During the Civil War

Dan Fleming

From early on in the Civil War, newspapers played a central role in the opinions and decisions people made. In Newark, the *Advocate* was a strong Democratic paper, while the *North American* was known as a Republican and abolitionist paper. The two were always at each other's throats, reporting political activities, accusing and exaggerating. Even so, many partisan businessmen advertised in both.

The loyal following of the papers produced an interesting phenomenon during the war. People began giving gifts. On November 29, 1861, the *Advocate* reported: "Our thanksgiving turkey—one of the finest of the season,--came from our friend Mr. Absalom Hollar. He will accept our thanks for his kind remembrance."

On April 1, 1864 came the report of a suspicious package. It brought a response much like today with our threats of terrorism. The editor wrote, "Early this week, a stranger who said he came through St. Albans (a township where democrats' houses get burned,) brought to our office a mysterious looking package which on being unwrapped was found to contain a suspicious-looking canister, closely sealed and directed to the editor. Not liking its looks, and the bearer being unable to tell us who had sent it, or where it came from, we concluded to lay the thing away and not be in a hurry about opening it. Some hours later, however, a letter received through the post office, furnished the following sweet solution of the mystery."

That letter said, "Friend Morgan [the editor]—I send you

a sample of my maple sugar. I suppose that you would like to know how it comes that my hens lay sugar eggs. Well, the facts are these: I have the boys drive the hens into my sugar camp on Good Friday, and let them have all the maple sap that they can drink, and then about Easter we always have a fine lot of sugar eggs. I have made 600 pounds of sugar this season, besides what the hens have laid…Long life to you and a happy one. [signed] Jacob Row. Morgan replied, "We thank our good friend, Major Row, for his kind remembrance. Doubtless, his idea was that an editor has so many sour things to encounter, a little sweetening would not come amiss to him. He was right. The sugar is the handsomest we have seen in Newark, and the eggs are such noble ones that we are sure none but honest democratic hens could have produced them…"

In July 1864, the following noticed appeared: "We are indebted to our friend, Mr. J. B. Irwin, of Franklin township, for a bucket of the largest and sweetest dewberries we have seen this season. Mr. Irwin's blackberry patch yielded him last year seventy dollars; and he has already realized this season upwards of thirty dollars from the sale of dewberries." Perhaps the gifts came from an attempt to obtain free advertising!

On December 30, 1864, the *Advocate* printed, "We are indebted to some unknown friend for an exceedingly fine Christmas turkey sent to our house on Saturday last. Well stuffed and roasted, it was exceedingly palateable [sic]; but it would have tasted much sweeter had we known the friend to whom we were indebted for kind remembrance."

By mid-1864, the *Advocate* had to post reminders to subscribers to keep their accounts paid. Newsprint was getting not only expensive, but scarce, and was also being taxed. Perhaps that is why there are only a few issues available today for 1865.

Christmas

Dan Fleming

Christmas was not always the event that drove the general economy each year or had children expecting all of their gift wishes to come true. There were hints of that upcoming trend, though, in newspaper ads during the 1860s, although the letters home from the field generally did not mention the holiday.

In 1861 John Koos's Confectionery announced, "Santa Claus has arrived and left his budget of toys. And a finer display of good things and 'fancy fixins' never lit down in Newark before. As will be seen by the life size portrait in Koos's window the old man has a choice supply of wooden, tin and fancy toys for little folks, and since Koos has paid cash for them he intends to sell cheaper than can be bought any where in the city. Attention is also called to the large stock of candy toys manufactured by Koos himself and sold CHEAPER THAN EVER BEFORE, either at wholesale or retail. So let all the lovers of good things show their good taste in buying their tasty fixins for the holiday at Koos's Confectionery, one door east of the post office."

In 1862 an unusual, although practical, idea for a Christmas gift was advertised in the *Advocate*. "What more appropriate for a Holiday gift to your friend than a fine pair of Gold Spectacles combining utility, ornament and durability. Cadwell, the Optician, now at the Holton house, has some splendid ones, besides a large assortment of silver and other frames, the lenses of which are all of the purest quality. Such an opportunity as this to be properly suited with glasses is rarely offered to our citizens. Mr. C. remains another week only."

Also that year, a committee planned a holiday treat at City Hall on December 24 and 25 and the first weekend in January, although its description was rather vague:

"On these three evenings all are invited to attend and partake of the nice things prepared. Bands will be in attendance. Admission first night, 15 cents; the other nights, 25 cents."

In 1863, Koos combined his advertising with another business. "Toys for Holidays. Just now, the windows of Brennan and Koos are objects of considerable attraction to youngsters who are looking anxiously for the arrival of Christmas. These establishments are prepared to supply all the wants of community in the line of toys, candies, fruits, nuts, etc." The Atcherly & Son dry goods store announced that it would close for Christmas day, but they had a new supply of winter clothing. Newton & Keagy was offering "an elegant stock of Christmas goods which they feel sure will enable them to supply every want of their customers."

By 1864, Brennan had combined with Kuster to offer "an assortment of attractive toys for holiday gifts to the juveniles. In the book and album line, we also notice that both the old and new book store are well prepared to supply the wants of all who are flush with greenbacks and desire to present a kindly token to friend or acquaintance."

Curiously, there was an ad in 1864 for "Hasheesh Candy, the Oriental Nervine Compound, for the first time introduced into this country in a medicated and agreeable form." Some of the other language used to describe it was "exhilarant confectionized," "adds to beauty as well as years," "gladden the heart," "gather new inspiration," and "sold by druggists everywhere."

Dis worl' was made in jiss six days,
An' finish'd up in various ways;
Look away! look away! look away! Dixie Land!
Dey den made Dixie trim an' nice,
But Adam call'd it "Paradise."
Look away! look away! look away! Dixie Land!

– the original first stanza of *Dixie* by Daniel Decatur Emmett

HEROES ALL

John Lincoln Clem, shortly after the Battle of Chickamauga. From the collection of Licking County Library, donated by Columbus Metropolitan Library, 2002. The print is a reproduction of the original at the National Archives.

Johnny Clem – Boy of War

Linda A. Leffel

As Licking County citizens faced the realization that Civil War had begun in our divided nation, many anguished at the thought of loved ones leaving our community to fight, possibly never to return. But even with the fear of what lay ahead, a "buzz" grew around town as recruitment of area men began. Newark native, Captain Leonidas McDougal (spelled McDugall in military records), was one who led area recruitment and training. In no time, he had his quota filled with young men who felt the call of duty to their alienated nation.

But if fear gripped some, the thought of war meant excitement to others—such as 9-year-old Johnny Klem, fascinated by the thought of adventure and glamorized war. It is estimated that well over 10,000 boys under age 18 joined the Union Army during the Civil War—some only 13 or younger! Of these many "boys of war", our John Lincoln Clem (as he was later known, with spelling change) is one of the most famous of all.

John Joseph Klem was the first-born child of parents Roman and Magdalene Klem. Recently returning to Newark from living in Cincinnati, they stayed with relatives (the Kline family) at 26 W. Harrison Street at the time of Johnny's birth. For years, controversy has surrounded whether this was Johnny's birthplace, for the Klem name is not found on property or census records, as they did not own or rent property while living with the Kline's. Soon Roman would buy property at the corner of Granville and 11th Streets, where

Johnny spent his childhood.

Johnny was "big brother" to the only other children born to Roman and Magdalene who lived to adulthood—his sister, Mary Elizabeth (Lizzie) and brother, Louis. Accounts show Johnny was very close to his siblings. He felt even more responsibility for their care following the death of their mother, tragically struck down by a train. Johnny said "life will never be the same" following his beloved mother's death, although he soon loved the stepmother his father married. He had a typical childhood of school, church at St. Francis de Sales, playing and doing chores, but our adventurous Johnny did not seem to like school much. He felt destined for more exciting things!

So it would be this fascination with the war that would take Johnny from Newark. Many contradictions of his enlistment exist: pleading with his father (who of course said no) to join the troops; presenting himself to Capt. McDougal, who laughed at him; leaving Lizzie and Louis at church to run off with the 3rd Ohio; being noticed, sent back home, only to stow away again to "tag along" until too far from home to make him return; and finally, ending up with the 22nd Michigan unit. Unfortunately, many versions, including first-hand accounts, are conjecture with "holes" in their timing. But regardless, join he did! Among the youngest, he would not be officially mustered in until 1863 at age 11. As a sergeant by 12, he became the youngest to ever serve as an NCO in the US Army!

Dawes Arboretum and the American Civil War

Doug Stout

W hen you walk the trails of Dawes Arboretum, you would never guess that these idyllic surroundings had any connection with the Civil War. Beman Dawes and his wife, Bertie, founded the Arboretum in 1929. He was originally from Marietta and was the son of Rufus Dawes.

Rufus Dawes, a great grandson of William (Billie) Dawes who rode with Paul Revere, graduated from Marietta College and was working in Wisconsin when the Civil War started. He became a Lieutenant Colonel in the 6th Wisconsin Infantry, otherwise nicknamed the Iron Brigade for its "iron disposition in battle," or "black hats" because of the black Hardee hats they wore instead of the usual regulation kepi. The Iron Brigade's reputation as hard fighters was not just known among its comrades, but also its enemies. Its southern foes on the battlefield of Gettysburg were heard to say, "Here come those damned black hat fellers," knowing they were in for a fight!

With this group of men Rufus fought in some of the heaviest fighting of the eastern theater; Antietam, Fredericksburg, Chancellorsville, Gettysburg, The Wilderness, Cold Harbor. Dawes saw the war up close and personal as shown in a letter to his future wife, written three days after the battle of Gettysburg on July 6, 1863.

"This has been a terrible ordeal. Our loss is 30 killed outright, 116 wounded, several of whom have died since, and 25 missing, all from 340 men taken into battle. My horse was shot from under me early in the fight, which perhaps saved my life. The experience of the past few days seems more like a horrible dream than the reality. May God save me and my men from any more such trials. I could tell a thousand stories of their heroism: One young man, Corporal James Kelly of company 'B', shot through the breast, came staggering up to me before he fell and opening his shirt to show the wound, said 'Colonel, won't you write to my folks that I died a soldier.' Every man of our color guard was shot and several volunteer color bearers. There was not a man of them but would die before the honor of the old Sixth should be tarnished."

Beman's uncle, Rufus's brother, Ephraim Dawes, fought with the 53rd Ohio Volunteer Infantry. With the 53rd he was at Shiloh and Vicksburg, and during Sherman's march to Atlanta, he fought at Resaca and Dallas, Georgia. It was at Dallas that he received his wound that shot away the lower part of his jaw leaving him horribly disfigured and in extreme pain. He was honorably discharged and brevetted Lieutenant Colonel. It was said he once wrote that because of his wound he had not known one waking moment free of pain. Ephraim found some relief when a Cincinnati surgeon reconstructed his lower lip, jaw and teeth.

One has to wonder if after hearing and seeing his father's and uncle's war stories and wounds if Bemen Dawes' love for the peace and tranquility of nature wasn't somehow born out of the horrific conflict of the Civil War.

The French Brothers of Alexandria and the Battle of Ringgold

Dan Fleming

On November 27, 1863, one of the Union's greatest losses took place at Ringgold Gap, Georgia, also known as Taylor's Ridge. Union forces had routed the Confederates two days before at Missionary Ridge, Tennessee. Three divisions under Maj. Gen. Joseph Hooker pursued them to Ringgold Gap. Confederate Maj. Gen. Patrick Cleburne held the gap through the mountains for five hours with 4,100 troops against Hooker's 12,000. So many Union soldiers fell that one description compared them to house shingles lying over each other.

The 76th O.V.I. commanded by Maj. Willard Warner was the first unit on the scene at the top of the ridge, only to find the Confederates waiting for them over the crest. Within ten minutes, 18 men of the 76th were killed and 44 were wounded, including eight color-bearers. As each soldier holding the flag fell, another took his place. Wounded in this manner were William Montgomery, who lost an arm, Corp. Johnston Haughey, Sgt. George Preston and Lieutenants James Blackburn and John Metzger. Joseph Jennings and Capt. Ira P. French were killed. It was said that Maj. Warner himself held up the flag for a short while until he found another to take over.

There has been confusion over the years regarding the flag of the 76th in this battle. There were actually two flags. The national flag had "76th" sewn onto it. A photograph showing it in tatters may be seen on the cover of the book,

Frank D. French. From the *Newark Advocate*, June 5, 1939.

A Boy's Service with the 76th Ohio. This flag was never captured. The other one was the state regimental flag for the 76th, which sported a large eagle with outspread wings. This one was captured when its bearer, Silas Priest, was wounded. This is the one that was returned by the survivors of the 1st Arkansas at the 38th reunion ceremony of the 76th O.V.I. in Newark in 1916. Part of the confusion was due to the fact that the regimental flag was often called a banner by veterans who participated in the battle and by many subsequent articles.

Ira Paige French had been one of the first to enlist for three months with Capt. Leonidas McDougal's Co. H, 3rd O.V.I. Regiment. This unit was originally called the Wide Awakes as a local militia group. Once they were officially enlisted for service, they were nicknamed the Licking Tigers. After his three months were over with the 3rd, Ira helped recruit Company B of the 76th for three years. He was commissioned 1st Lieutenant in November 1861 and Captain in September 1862. He returned home in September 1863 to marry to a daughter of Deacon Rose, just three months before he was killed. His body was returned and buried at Maple Grove Cemetery in Alexandria.

Ira's brother, Frank Douglas French, witnessed his death in the battle. In 1937, Frank wrote details of this to *Advocate* writer, Minnie Hite Moody. Frank has the distinction of being the last survivor of the Civil War in Licking County. He died June 4, 1939 at 95 years old.

The father of Ira and Frank was Truman B. French, who had come to Ohio from New York in 1813. He married Rosetta M. Paige in Granville in 1828 and became the first superintendent of the Licking County Infirmary in 1838. He relocated to Johnstown in 1849, where he ran a hotel for two years. Truman died on October 8, 1863, less than two months before his son, Ira, was killed.

Private John W. Gardner
76th Ohio Volunteer Infantry, Company A

Larry Stevens

John W. Gardner was born in Fallsbury Township, Licking County, Ohio, on April 5, 1843. As a youngster he attended the district school and worked on the family farm until he was almost nineteen years of age. With the wave of patriotism sweeping the North, he entered the service of his country in October 1861 by enlisting in Captain Thaddeus Lemert's Company A, 76th Ohio Volunteer Infantry Regiment. The company was sworn into United States service at Camp Sherman in Newark, Ohio, located at what is today known as the Great Circle Mound.

While serving with the 76th, the young Gardner fought in many small skirmishes and engagements, plus the more major battles at Fort Donelson, Shiloh, Corinth, Arkansas Post, Vicksburg, Lookout Mountain, Ringgold Gap, and the battles for Atlanta, Jonesboro, and the Carolinas Campaign.

This "Billy Yank" was wounded in the left wrist and hand in a desperate fight at Ringgold Gap near Chattanooga on November 27, 1863. Following recovery he returned to action and then, some ten months later at Jonesboro during the Atlanta fighting, Gardner received a second gunshot wound, this time to the upper left arm. While in recuperation he missed Sherman's "March to the Sea." Healed, he caught up to the regiment at Hilton Head, S.C. in December 1864. He went on to participate in the Carolinas Campaign, which ended with the surrender on April 26, 1865, of Gen. Joseph Johnston's CSA army to Gen. William T. Sherman's

Private John W. Gardner.
From the collection of Larry Stevens.

Union army, which included the Ohio 76th. This was the largest troop surrender of the war. With the war over, the victorious Northern Armies were marched to Washington, D.C. where they participated on May 23-24, 1865, in a two-day Grand Review of the Army down Pennsylvania Avenue. John Gardner recalled this special day the rest of his life.

Following his discharge after the end of the war, John returned to Licking County and resumed his pre-war occupation of farming. He married Lenora Denman in 1869, and the couple had eight children. After the death of Lenora in 1901, John married Lucretia B. Mitchell.

In compensation for his injuries received during the war, Gardner was granted a government pension of $8 per month. He took an active role in local politics and followed the Republican Party. This veteran "Boy in Blue" served as a proud member of the Grand Army of the Republic, Evans Post #668 located in the village of Elizabethtown, now called Perryton. This post #668 was named in honor of fellow 76th O.V.I. member, Captain Zebulon P. Evans who commanded a company in the Regiment. Old soldier John W. Gardner passed away on October 8, 1925 at the age of 82, and is buried at Perryton Cemetery.

Leonidas Hamaline Inscho
Licking County's 1st Medal of Honor Recipient

E. Chris Evans

The Medal of Honor is America's highest award for military valor. It is bestowed only upon those who have performed an act of such conspicuous gallantry as to rise "above and beyond the call of duty." Licking County is blessed to have on its rolls two recipients for their Civil War service.

The first recipient was Leonidas H. Inscho who was born on February 20, 1840 at Chatham, the eldest son of Moses and Ada (Preston) Inscho. On June 21, 1861, shortly after war broke out between the states, Leonidas rode to Newark and volunteered for service in Co. "E," 12th Ohio Volunteer Regiment.

Inscho was promoted from Private to Corporal, to Sergeant, to 1st Sergeant and finally to the rank of 2nd Lieutenant. Transferred to the 23rd Ohio Volunteer Infantry Regiment, Leonidas served along side two fellow officers of the 23rd who both later became President of the United States, Rutherford B. Hayes and William McKinley. Inscho was wounded three times while fighting in the major battles of South Mountain, at Antietam, and at both Winchester and Cedar Creek in the Shenandoah Valley.

At the Battle of South Mountain, Maryland, on September 14, 1862, Leonidas' actions led to his designation as Medal of Honor recipient. Left behind on the battlefield by his regiment when an enemy bullet smashed his rifle and wounded his left hand, he soon found himself face to face with a Rebel Captain and five of his men who demanded his sur-

render. Single hand-
edly, he wrestled the
Captain's revolver
away and captured
the officer and four
of his men, finding it
necessary to kill the
sixth Confederate in
the process. A reli-
gious man, Inscho

Grave marker, Cedar Hill Cemetery, Newark, Ohio. Photo by Aaron Keirns.

justified the shooting as "it was my life or his'n."

Following the war, Leonidas Inscho returned to Licking County and the family farm. For 16 years he operated a grist-mill and sawmill in Chatham. In January 1870, he married Laura Maria McKinney. In 1883, the family moved to Newark where Leonidas operated a profitable grocery. He joined Lemert Post G.A.R., Acme Lodge #534 F&AM, and served as Chairman of the Committee that approved the plans for the Soldiers and Sailors Memorial Building. In 1892, In-scho's old friend Governor William McKinley, appointed him Commandant of the military training grounds at the Octagon Mound with the rank of Captain. Here, annual summer training took place for Ohio National Guard and Militia troops from 1892 to 1903.

The Inscho family belonged to the Methodist Episcopal Church where Leonidas served as Sunday School Superintendent. On November 12, 1907, this hero succumbed to cancer of the jaw and is buried at Cedar Hill Cemetery. His Medal of Honor is today the property of, and displayed by the Licking County Historical Society.

Let it be said that he was just a common man, but a man of uncommon valor and bravery in the service of his country – Leonidas Hamaline Inscho, Licking County's first Medal of Honor recipient.

The Lemert Family

Dan Fleming

In the northeast corner of Licking County rests the small village of Perryton, just off State Route 586. It was settled in 1817 by Elizabeth Glasscock Lemert, who called it Elizabethtown. She had moved there from Virginia with her family of six boys and a girl after her husband died. Those children grew up and gave Elizabeth many grandchildren, thirteen of whom fought for the Union in the Civil War.

Thaddeus Lemert recruited for Col. Charles R. Woods and was commissioned a 2nd Lieutenant of the 76th O.V.I., Co. A. He led 41 recruits into Camp Sherman after hosting an ice cream party by lamplight. He fought at Fort Donelson, Shiloh, Corinth and Vicksburg, then was killed at Arkansas Post in January 1863. His brother, Orren, heard his last words: "Our forefathers died for their country—why should not I?"

After that battle, Orren was sent to Mississippi to raise a company of black soldiers, becoming the Captain of the 51st U.S. Colored Troops regiment. He survived the war and moved to Kansas afterward, then to Texas.

Orren's younger brother, Laban, joined the 76th as a private, but was moved to the 51st as a 1st Sergeant to serve under Orren. He was later promoted to 2nd Lieutenant. He, too, moved to Kansas after the war.

Beverly W. and George L. (brothers) enlisted with Co. A of the 76th O.V.I., Beverly as a 1st Lieutenant. He was promoted to Captain in 1862, although his cousin, Thaddeus, was still commanding the company. He was probably being groomed by Col. Woods to lead another unit. He went to Kansas after the war and ended up in Montana. George worked with the Field and Staff company, but was transferred into the Regimental Band. He was mustered out in August 1862 as an invalid and died in 1872.

Another set of brothers was John A., Nathan F., Thomas J. and Edward L. Lemert. John was with Co. A of the 76th and was wounded at Ringgold Gap on November 27, 1863. He died four days later. Nathan was with Co. D of the 22nd O.V.I. under Capt. Homer Thrall of Granville. While his regiment was in St. Louis in November 1861, he contracted typhoid. His mother travelled there just in time to hold his hand as he died. She brought his body home for burial at Perryton Cemetery. Thomas joined the 135th Ohio National Guard and was captured with many from that company and sent to Andersonville Prison. He died of scurvy in September 1864. Edward enlisted while attending Hiram College at age 16, recruited by the college president, Col. James A. Garfield. He was wounded, captured and exchanged, becoming the only one of his brothers to survive the war. He moved to Oklahoma where he died in 1933.

Charles C. was a drummer boy for Co. A., 76th O.V.I.. He was wounded at Arkansas Post on the same day his cousin, Thaddeus, was killed. Charles died a few days later. His brother, George A. was a Captain of the 97th O.V.I. from Muskingum County. He survived and moved out to Kansas by 1885.

George W. enlisted with Co. A of the 87th O.V.I. while attending Marietta College, but only for four months. He and his family later settled in Columbus, Ohio.

Elizabeth's daughter, Minerva, married William S. Brown and had a son, Jay H. Brown. Jay served with Co. A, 76th as a musician, survived the war, but died in 1867.

Marker at the Battle of Arkansas Post, where Thaddeus Lemert was Killed.

Photo by Dan Fleming.

The spot in the Arkansas River where northern gunboats fired upon Fort Hildeman at the Battle of Arkansas Post.

Photo by Dan Fleming.

When the Lemert Post #71 of the G.A.R. (Grand Army of the Republic) was formed in 1881, it was named after Captain Thaddeus Lemert.

Abstracted from "The Lemert Family in the Civil War" in the *Licking Valley Ledger*, July 2011 by the same author.

Note: This story was partially written as a promotional article for the Perryton Cemetery Walk on October 2, 2011, sponsored by the Licking Valley Heritage Society. It highlighted six Civil War soldiers plus Elizabeth Glasscock Lemert who founded the village of Elizabethtown (later called Perryton) and had 13 grandsons in the war.

Captain Cary M. Marriott

Larry Stevens

Cary M. Marriott was the son of Thomas and Drusilla Marriott of Eden Township in Licking County. The family name was sometimes spelled "Merriott" as in the U.S. Census of 1860, or even Merritt in the 1850 Census. Cary was the oldest of eight children, the others being Mary Ann, Madison H., Greenbury J., Francis Marion, Bowen Hill, Elmus W. and Randolph.

Captain Cary M. Marriott.
From the collection of Larry Stevens.

Cary enlisted in the 76th Ohio Volunteer Infantry, Company D as a sergeant. He was promoted to 2nd lieutenant on November 24, 1863 and 1st Lieutenant on March 10, 1864. Then on June 16, 1865 he was made a captain. In the 76th, he served on the staff of General Charles R. Woods, and was considered a "brave and stylish officer." He was mustered out with the regiment in 1865.

After the war, Cary married Emma. By 1870 the family was living in Alabama, where they stayed throughout their lives. Their children were Alice, Edward, Cary, Mary, Henderson and Frank. Cary and Emma disappeared from the Census as of 1920.

Major Charles Dana Miller
and the Florida Land Scheme

Dan Fleming

This story is well known in Florida, but may not be so in Licking County. Charles Dana Miller was born in Mt. Vernon, Ohio on September 3, 1836, the son of James and Anna Gilman Miller. After a good education and some travel, he moved to Newark at the age of 21 and worked with Luke K. Warner in the grain business.

Miller enlisted in the Civil War on October 18, 1861 with the 76th Ohio Volunteer Infantry under Captain Levi P. Coman of Company C. He worked his way up the ranks, being promoted to Captain of Company C in 1864. He left the service on November 18, 1864 and was breveted to major by the President in 1867. He was wounded slightly in the foot at Vicksburg and in the hip at Resaca, but did not report the wounds. His service included all of the engagements the 76th encountered up to the date of his mustering out.

Miller enjoyed painting, drawing, landscape gardening and geology. He married Lucy Gilman Jewett in May 1865, but she died in 1869, leaving two children. He remarried sometime afterward and had five more children.

He was secretary of the committee that organized the huge reunion of the Soldiers and Sailors of Licking County veterans group at the "Old Fort" (Great Circle Mound) in 1878. Present were President Hayes, General Garfield, General W. T. Sherman and General Willard Warner. 121 battle flags were on display and 179 Ohio regiments were represented. After the reunion, Miller produced a detailed book of over 300 pages of all the proceedings and speeches, plus a comprehensive list of Licking County veterans who had died up through 1878.

In the late 1880's, according to his obituary, Miller went to Florida to improve his health. This is the only mention in Licking County sources of his connection with Florida, but it turns out he was very busy there. He persuaded many Union veterans and others, many from Licking County, to invest in a new community called Federal Hill, about 17 miles southwest of Jacksonville. It was laid out with 36 squares of four acres, each having eight lots. In the center was a square, much like in Newark, called Lincoln Park. The plan provided for wide streets, schools, churches and the G.A.R.

The investors used the development of southern California as a model and claimed that Florida was entering a new period of prosperity and growth as a health resort. He published a 25 page prospectus outlining the area's history, climate, crops, wildlife, etc., which could be the envy of today's developers.

Local folks did not appreciate his efforts, however. It was said he flaunted his Union background and boasted of the 76th O.V.I.'s exploits through Georgia. It seemed to them like another invasion of the South by the North, profiting by their misfortune.

Ironically, by the 1940's there was nothing left of the community but a cemetery and a couple of telegraph poles. It might have been the two hard freezes that killed the citrus in 1894 and 1895, or the yellow fever epidemic in 1897. Whatever the reason, the neighbors of Federal Hill were glad to see its demise.

Major David A. B. Moore

Dan Fleming

David A. B. Moore of Newark was already a war veteran by the time the Civil War began. He had enlisted in 1847 for the war with Mexico under Capt. John R. Duncan. Their 100-man unit was known as "Duncan's Mounted Rangers," and Moore was its first lieutenant. They rode from Newark to Cincinnati on their own horses, where they boarded a steamer called *Star Spangled Banner*, bound for New Orleans. Another steamer took them to the mouth of the Rio Grande. Near there, they spent their time on guard duty and delivering mail and dispatches, while dodging guerilla gun fire. They were mustered out on August 2, 1848.

Moore was born October 8, 1821, the only son of Moses Moore, and nephew of David Moore who founded the Mary Ann Furnace. He followed his father in the cabinet-making trade and lived in Newark with his wife, Elizabeth Cross. After the Mexican War, he served two terms as a justice of the peace.

In June 1861, D. A. B. Moore, as he was known then, was chairman of the Licking County Democratic Convention. By July, he was ordered to raise a cavalry company, and he became Captain of the First Ohio Volunteer Cavalry, Company D. They left Newark in early August and were mustered in at Camp Chase in Columbus on October 5. They enjoyed an oyster dinner at camp for Thanksgiving on November 23, where Moore and two lieutenants of the company were presented with dress swords and belts.

Moore wrote home from Camp Buell near Louisville,

Major David A. B. Moore.
From the collection of the
Licking Co. Historical Society.

Kentucky, the day after Christmas 1861, where they had spent a week breaking mules. His personal goal at that time was to confiscate all the alcohol he could find in camp. He said, "If the whiskey makers will send all their whiskey to the rebels, and allow none to our troops, we will end the war and be home by the 4th of July, as it is more effective in its aim than rifles."

At the end of March 1862, Moore was ill and confined to his room in Nashville. He related in a letter about how reduced in numbers all the companies were, due to casualties, illness, detachments for assignments, and AWOL's. His was down to 54, and Capt. Putnam had but 39 rank and file left. By September, Moore was feeling better and marched back to Louisville. He said, "The boys are in good spirits. We marched near forty hours without so much as a cracker." He was present at the Battle of Perryville on October 8, 1862 and witnessed the death of Capt. Leonidas McDougal.

Moore's turn came on December 29, 1862 at the battle of Stone River, where the first bullet fired struck his saddle horn and threw a fragment into his forehead. The *Advocate* reported on January 16, 1863 that Moore had been promoted to Major just ten days before his death. A later report said he lived four days after being shot, dying at a Confederate hospital in Murfreesboro, Tennessee. His body was returned to Newark for burial at Cedar Hill Cemetery. All businesses in town closed for the service. He was so respected that his photograph was later placed into the cornerstone of the Soldiers and Sailors Memorial Building (later known as the Auditorium Theater) on June 11, 1894.

Capt. John H. Putnam

Dan Fleming

Most Ohioans know of General Rufus Putnam, Revolutionary War General and U.S. Surveyor General who helped establish the Ohio Company to settle Ohio. He was also instrumental in preventing slavery in Ohio.

One of his many grandsons was John H. Putnam, born in 1835 in Springfield, Ohio. By 1860, he and his brother, Rufus, were in Newark, operating a printing business. John was civic-minded, like many of his ancestors, so on June 10th, 1861, he proposed that Newark hold an old-fashioned 4th of July celebration. Many people from all the townships formed a committee to organize the event. They elected Putnam as secretary of the group, and as Grand Marshal.

Putnam printed a Democratic paper called the *Voice of the People*, so he knew the value of advertising. On August 23, 1861, he ran an ad in the *Advocate* saying he was given authority from Columbus to recruit an infantry company for 3-year's service. By late September, his Company H was filled and attached to Col. Moses B. Walker's 31st Regiment O.V.I.. They trained at Camp Dick Robinson in Kentucky. A letter home in November described mule-breaking and a huge military ball. He tactfully explained that "the Kentucky ladies are much overrated for beauty, and will not compare with the girls we left behind us."

Putnam experienced a few skirmishes on his march to Corinth, Mississippi, but avoided a battle, because the city was already evacuated. Back at Perryville, Kentucky, he was under fire but not actively engaged. He had an encounter with Morgan's Raiders on November 20, 1862, and captured a couple of "Morganites," as he put it, on the 23rd. Then came the battle of Murfreesboro, also called Stones River. On January 6, 1863 he wrote an extremely detailed, day-by-day report on the battle from December 30 to January 3, 1863. In his gruesome and graphic description, which spoke glowingly of General Rosecrans, he said, "Never do I wish to visit another battlefield."

Waldo Taylor (Mayor of Newark, 1884-85) wrote in 1863 that Putnam "pledged himself to his friends and the community before he went into the service that if the war assumed any other shape than for the restoration of the Union, that he would leave the service." In Putnam's letter of December 12, 1862 he had ranted about the upcoming Emancipation Proclamation: "Thousands of soldiers would leave the service if they could, and hundreds of officers will resign...if the Emancipation Proclamation is enforced..." It did take effect on January 1, 1863. Whether it was the memory of Murfreesboro or his Copperhead political views, Putnam resigned his commission, effective February 2, 1863, claiming ill health from rheumatism, although he led a very active life after that.

In the spring of 1863, he opened a store with James R. Atcherly on the south side of the Square, selling hats, boots, shoes and hosiery. Then he ran for Ohio Representative and won, serving from 1863-1866. He married Ella Gertrude Ewing in Ross County in 1867 and became editor of the *Chillicothe Advertiser* in 1872. He purchased the *Columbus Dispatch* in 1874, becoming its second owner. Putnam died in Chillicothe on December 23, 1892, leaving his wife and a daughter, Eveline.

Marcus Root and the Bullet

Ted Tower

Noble and Demaris Root, with son Alanson and daughter Belinda, moved to Licking County from Westfield, Massachusetts in 1807 and took up land southeast of Granville. In 1854 Alanson moved with his wife, Phebe, and ten children to Harrison Township, where by 1861 they were a reasonably successful family of sheep farmers. They had five sons of military age: Moses, Elias, Martin Luther, George, and Marcus, although Marcus was not 18 years old until March 1862. In that detail Marcus had a lot of company; many hot-blooded young men, anxious for glory on the battlefield, were just "rising 18" and not quite old enough, but there were ways around this trifling administrative detail, and many 16- and 17-year-olds found them. One of the most popular was to write the number "18" on a scrap of paper and put it in a shoe. Then when the recruiting officer asked how old the applicant was, he answered, "I'm over 18."

In the fall of 1861, Captain Charles R. Woods was authorized to recruit a regiment – the 76th Ohio Volunteer Infantry – from Licking and surrounding counties. Included in the seven companies from Licking County were Moses and Marcus Root. The 76th was mustered into U.S. service on February 9, 1862, with Woods in command, and immediately "took the cars" (transportation by rail) for Paducah, Kentucky. It was then loaded onto steamboat transports and sailed up the Cumberland River in time to fight under General U.S. Grant in the Battle of Fort Donelson. The 76th then went on to fight at Shiloh, Corinth and Milliken's Bend, all in 1862, served with honor in a total of 44 battles, and was mustered out as the 76th Veteran Volunteer Infantry on July 15, 1865.

Moses Barrett Root served the entire war and was mustered out as a corporal, all without having received a scratch, but for 17-year-old Marcus there is a different story. The roster of the 76th shows that Marcus was mustered in, but there is no further word, and he

Marcus Root.
From the collection of Ted Tower.

does not appear as mustered out in July 1865. Somewhere during those first battles in 1862, Marcus was shot.

According to family legend, Marcus received a wound which was serious enough to remove him from the battle. While he was waiting for help to arrive, he kept himself busy by digging the bullet that shot him out of the tree behind him. He succeeded, because help was a long time coming in the serious battles. At his first opportunity, he sent the bullet to his older brother, Elias, for safekeeping. This relic of a young man's first experience with the glories of battle remains with Elias Root's descendents yet today.

There is a suggestion of corroboration to this legend, besides the obvious fact of the mangled and blood-stained bullet in the family archives. In the summer and fall of 1862, the Ellet Brothers of Cairo, Illinois, recruited marines for their fleet of steam rams. Since men were scarce and the Army needed all it could get, the Ellet's were allowed to recruit from

Bullet removed from Marcus Root, in the Tower family collection.

among recuperating wounded in the hospitals of St. Louis, Missouri. Marcus Root's discharge, which recently came to light, shows that he enlisted in the Mississippi Marine Brigade in March 1863, and was discharged in January 1865.

Marcus married Elizabeth Williams and moved first to Robinson, Illinois and then to Merom, Indiana, where he became a mail carrier. His wife died in 1917. Marcus was struck and killed by an automobile in Miami, Florida in 1920, where he was visiting an old Army buddy. He and his wife are buried in the old cemetery at Robinson, Illinois.

William Starke Rosecrans,

Distinguished General from Homer, Ohio

D. Robert Tharp

Welliam Rosecrans (1818-1898) was born in southern Kingston Township of Delaware County just north of Sunbury, Ohio. His birthplace and early childhood home was located on Rosecrans Road (Township Road 69). Today, the site is marked with a large stone and memorial plaque, surrounded by an iron fence.

William was the second of five sons. His father, Crandall, fought in the War of 1812, where he served as an adjutant to General William Henry Harrison. His mother, Jemima Hopkins, could trace her lineage back to Stephen Hopkins, Governor of Rhode Island, and a signer of the Declaration of Independence.

The Rosecrans family moved to Homer, Ohio when William was a small child. Around the age of five, long before he became a soldier or general, he engaged in his first battle, the Battle of Fort Homer. He was told to drive the neighbor's gander out of their garden, but the gander refused to go. The battle intensified, and William accidently killed it. Horrified, he took the dead gander to his neighbor. The lady forgave him and sent him home with bread and jam.

William's education was limited, but he was very intelligent. As a child he could recite the entire Declaration of Independence. Later, he attended the Martinsburg Academy at Martinsburg, Ohio and then applied and was admitted to the Military Academy at West Point where he excelled, graduating in 1842 as fifth in his class. At his graduation he met, fell in love with, and, in 1843, married Anna Hegeman.

Rosecrans was appointed a General in the volunteer army and was quite successful at the battles of Rich Mountain, Iuka, Corinth, and the Tullahoma Campaign. He was the hero of Stone River. In 1863, however, he was soundly defeated at the Battle of Chickamauga. He was relieved of his command, but later succeeded in driving the Confederates out of Missouri.

After the war, Rosecrans served as Minister to Mexico. Upon returning home he was asked to run for governor of Ohio in 1866 and again in 1869, but he declined. Instead, he moved to California and bought 16,000 acres in the Los Angeles area. He was elected to the U. S. House of Representatives where he served from 1881 through 1885. Later, he was appointed Register of the Treasury. During this time, the image of Martha Washington appeared on the one dollar silver certificate, the only time a woman's image has appeared on U.S. paper currency. The signature, "W.S. Rosecrans, Register of the Treasury," appeared beneath her picture.

In 1893, he resigned due to poor health, and returned to California where he lived until his death on March 11, 1898. He was buried at Los Angeles until arrangements could be made for re-interment, with military honors, at Arlington National Cemetery. He was re-interred on May 17, 1902. President Theodore Roosevelt spoke at the service.

Abstracted from an article written by D. Robert Tharp, LCHS Trustee, for the Spring 2011 *Licking County Historical Society Quarterly*.

Captain Homer Thrall

Martha Sturgill

"Ho, For the War! Our Country Expects Every Man to Do His Duty!" This is the type of call to enlist that Homer Thrall, son of a miller/ farmer, would have answered in 1861 at the age of 29. Born in Granville on October 27, 1832 to Linus Thrall (a former native of Vermont) and Lucy Wolcott Thrall, he accepted a Captaincy in Company B of the 17th O.V.I.. After serving his 90 days with them, he enlisted for three years with Company D of the 22nd O.V.I. beginning in November 1861. Homer had attended Licking County public schools and then graduated from Kenyon College in Gambier. Most probably he earned this Captaincy for recruiting men to serve under him from the Alexandria and Granville vicinity. At the time of his enlistment, he lived in Alexandria, Ohio.

This could have been about all we know about Captain Thrall, were it not for Miss Emma Boudinot. She was the daughter of Elisha and Henrietta Mundy Boudinot, natives of Liverpool, England and members of the Congregational Church in Alexandria. Homer and Emma corresponded throughout the war. The letters survived and copies were donated to the Alexandria Museum in February 2011 by Linda Stewart of St. Charles, Illinois.

Because of these letters we know that Captain Thrall, in addition to being a dutiful officer, yearned for hearth and home. On March 30th, 1862 he wrote from Pittsburg Landing, Tennessee:

"Emma, every day but increases my love for you and I

come to consider you as near and dear to me as though you were my wife and not merely my betrothed. And I never have a doubt but that you and I will not long hence be united in holy wedlock."

We also get a glimpse of some of the hardships experienced by soldiers in the field. In his June 10th, 1862 letter from near Booneville, Mississippi after the Battle of Shiloh, Homer writes:

"...I will write you a few lines again just to inform you that I have passed safely through the siege of Corinth, the only injury I received being the loss of whole night's sleep. Since the evacuation we have come to this place about 20 or 25 miles south of Corinth. We are rather short of transportation and consequently have our baggage with us but little of the time, not enough to have a change of clean clothes with me as often as I would like. We sleep most of the time under trees in the woods and a large portion of the time have nothing to eat but salt pork broiled on a stick and a hard cracker washed down with a little coffee in a tin cup. This is not very luxurious or wholesome but a soldier must put up with it."

We hear his sense of humor in the June 26th letter from the same location:

"You would smile to see my domicile. I have a piece of canvas about twelve feet wide and twenty feet long. I set two forks in the ground, place a pole across the top of them and stretch the canvas over that, fastening each end to stakes in the ground. You see I do not have to open any doors or windows in order to get a sufficiency of fresh air. I have all that is around. Sometimes when it rains I get rather more than my share but that does not do much harm to a soldier, in fact cold water is rather beneficial than otherwise...."

Emma and Homer were married in 1863 and had three children: Linus G., Josephine and Eloise. Homer was mustered out of the Army in November 1864 as a Lieutenant Colonel with a creditable military record. After the war he moved to Columbus, Ohio and embarked on a second career, studying for the ministry and being ordained in the Congregational Church. He returned to Alexandria at least once for a reunion ceremony of Civil War veterans where he was asked to speak and pray.

In 1893, he entered his third and final career. He moved to Wyandot County and bought a weekly journal, *The Carey Times*. In Carey, Ohio Homer stood for reform and advancement "supporting in the columns of his paper all progressive public enterprises." (*Past and Present of Wyandot County, Ohio*, p. 249). Though a Democrat himself, he was viewed as impartial and fair in his editorship.

Who Held Lincoln's Head?

James P. Lukens and Dan Fleming

There is an old legend in Newark that her own John Veach was present during the shooting of President Abraham Lincoln by John Wilkes Booth, and that Veach held Lincoln's head in the theater. Veach was serving as inspector of military passes in Ford's Theater during the close of the Civil War in 1865. At the time, he was sitting with Major White in the rear of the theater. They were among the first people to assist the President. While rushing to the box, Veach saw the assassin Booth wave a dagger and cry, "Sic Semper Tyrannous," then jump from the box rail to the stage. He saw Booth catch his spurred left foot in the flag which draped the box, and saw clearly that Booth was injured.

It was Veach and Major White who carried Lincoln across the courtyard that separated the theater from the private residence where Lincoln lingered nearly 24 hours before he was relieved by death.

All the words above are drawn from an account published by the late W. Thomas Huff in his *Memories of Old Newark*, and submitted to us by James P. Lukens. Unfortunately, there is room for doubt.

First, by Huff's account, Veach was telling the story at the age of 75 while at the pension office applying for an increase, although he was described as yet mentally bright.

Second, the source cited by Huff (*Newark Advocate*, March 26, 1901) cannot be located now to verify the account. The newspaper exists on microfilm, but the account is not there. There might have been a typographical error with the date.

Third, if the Major White referred to above was the same one who commanded the 12th Ohio Volunteer Infantry, Company E in which Veach had enlisted, Veach should have known that by the time of Lincoln's assassination, White had moved up the ranks. In fact, White was breveted to brigadier general about a month before the assassination. Would Veach still have referred to him as "Major" and would White have been sitting in the back of Ford's Theater with Veach? Perhaps, but not likely.

Fourth, Veach's name has not been found in any other account of the tragedy, except by his own telling, nor has that of White. In fact, a very detailed account in the book, *Twenty Days*, by Dorothy and Philip Kunhardt describes how Dr. Charles Augustus Leale was the first on the scene, soon assisted by Dr. Charles Sabin Taft. Leale had been seated just 40 feet away. Then actress, Laura Keene, appeared with a pitcher of water and was allowed, even by the normally jealous Mrs. Lincoln, to hold the President's head in her lap. Two other doctors arrived. The four doctors and unnamed others slowly carried Lincoln out of the theater. Perhaps Veach was one of the unnamed others, but yet, it was Dr. Leale who held Lincoln's head at that point.

John F. Veach lived on 20 acres about two miles southeast of Newark. He enlisted in May 1861 with the 12th Ohio, Company E as a private for three months, then reenlisted with the same unit for three years and remained with it throughout the war. His service began under Colonel John W. Lowe, who was replaced by Major Carr B. White after Lowe was killed, White then being promoted to Colonel. They joined the Army of the Potomac on August 15, 1862 and participated in the battles at Bull Run, South Mountain, Antietam and Cloyd's Mountain. Veach and White were both mustered out on July 11, 1864.

Charles Robert Woods,

Brevet Major General, U. S. Army

E. Chris Evans

He died on February 26, 1885 in the same family home, Woodside, in which he was born some 58 years and 7 days before. Located at the north end of a long farm lane (which is today Newark's Woods Avenue), the site of the ancestral farm has served over the years as a family home, a public school and a digital academy. Licking County native Charles R. Woods, from the time he entered West Point in 1848 until he retired from the U.S. Army in 1874 and returned to Woodside, led a most exciting and successful military life.

In a nutshell, we can catalog his military career by pointing out that he served on the frontier after graduation and later was transferred to Washington, D. C. for garrison duty. When the Civil War commenced in April 1861, Woods was promoted to the rank of Colonel and assigned to the command of Newark's 76th Volunteer Infantry Regiment, leading it in the Mississippi River battles and the siege of Vicksburg. A promotion to the rank of Brigadier General followed, and he served as a brigade commander at Chattanooga and during Sherman's Atlanta Campaign and the "March to the Sea." Brevetted as a Major General for meritorious service, he led a division in the 15th Army Corps during the Carolina Campaign.

Following the end of the war, Woods remained in the Regular Army serving in the West and in Indian fighting. Because of failing health, he retired in 1874 as Colonel of

Shall Licking County raise a Regiment!

HO, FOR THE WAR!

Our Country expects every man to do his duty.

I HAVE been transferred from the regular army of the United States to the Ohio Volunteers, and am authorized by the Governor to raise and take command of the 76th regiment, which will go into camp at the Fair Grounds, near Newark. The men will be sworn in as fast as recruited, and their pay will commence immediately. The following recruiting officers have been appointed and the men recruited by them will be mustered into the 76th Regiment, to-wit:

CHARLES H. KIBLER,
L. P. COMAN,
H. O. KNOOP,
THADDEUS LEMERT,
JOSEPH M. SCOTT,
R. W. BURT.

I call upon the young men of my native county of Licking, and of the adjoining counties to fill up the ranks of a regiment which will be composed of their neighbors and friends. Your country in its extremest peril demands your services. This is the day and hour for patriotic young men to show their devotion to the cause of their country and its priceless institutions. Rally, then, under the banner which represents the Constitution and the Union, and symbols the honor and glory of our country at home and abroad. Crowd around the old flag which has secured to us all the blessings of free government, menaced as it now is by ingrates and rebels, resolved to maintain it to the last; and

"With arm to strike and soul to dare," protect it from insult, and carry it forward in triumph until "its sky-born glories burn" on every hill and in every valley of our beloved land.　　　　　　CHARLES R. WOODS, Col. commanding the 76th Reg. O. V. U. S. A.

Newark, O., Oct. 11, 1861.—tf11

Recruiting ad. The *Newark Advocate*, Oct. 26, 1861, p. 3.

the 2nd U.S. Infantry.

Yet, despite that impressive background, what set Charles Woods' military career apart from dozens of other fellow officers, were two incidents. He commanded the 200-man reinforcement, along with military supplies and food, which was aboard the side-wheeler steamship, *Star of the West*. Sent by President Buchanan in early January 1861 to relieve Fort Sumter, the unarmed ship was hit several times by Confederate cannon fire at Charleston harbor, and the civilian captain decided to return to New York City. As Major Robert Anderson, Union commander of Fort Sumter, wrote to the Governor of South Carolina, it was necessary "to regard this as an act of war." It was the first such overt act of what was to become the American Civil War.

Over four years later, division commander, Major General Charles Woods, was serving with Major General William T. Sherman in North Carolina when Confederate General Joe Johnston surrendered his army on April 26, 1865. This was the largest troop surrender of the war. Thus, Charles Woods has the unique distinction of being present and commanding men when both the first hostile act of war occurred, and at the end—indeed the Alpha and the Omega of the war.

William Burnham Woods,
Civil War General and U. S. Supreme Court Justice

D. Robert Tharp

William B. Woods has the distinction of being one of six Civil War generals from Licking County, and the only person from Licking County who has ever served on the United States Supreme Court.

Brevet Major General William B. Woods.
From the collection of Aaron Keirns.

He was born in Newark, Ohio on August 3, 1824. His father, Ezekiel Woods, an early pioneer of Licking County, came here from Kentucky in 1818. Ezekiel, and his wife Sarah, who was born in Zanesville, had four children. William's younger brother, Charles Robert, was also a Civil War general.

William attended Case Western Reserve for three years before transferring to Yale University for his senior year. He graduated with honors in 1845. In 1883, Yale University conferred upon him the honorary degree of "Doctor of Laws." After graduation, William returned to Newark and studied law in the firm of Samuel King. He was admitted to the Ohio bar in 1847. He married Anne Warner of Granville in 1855, and was elected Mayor of Newark that fall. He served in that office in 1856-57 before being elected to the Ohio House of Representatives, and eventually Speaker of the House.

In September, 1861 William joined the army, where he was appointed Lieutenant Colonel of the 76th Ohio Volunteer Infantry. He fought in numerous battles and skirmishes including Fort Donelson, Pittsburg Landing, Chickasaw Bayou, Arkansas Post (where he was slightly wounded), Resaca, Dallas, Atlanta, Jonesboro, Lovejoy Station, and Bentonville. He took part in the sieges of Vicksburg and Jackson. Under General William T. Sherman he was a part of the famous "March to the Sea" that destroyed all the towns and cities between Atlanta and Savannah, Georgia. He was mustered out of the Union Army in 1866 with the full rank of Brigadier General and Brevet Major General.

After the war, William left Ohio and moved to Alabama where he practiced law, purchased a cotton plantation, invested in an iron works and went into the lumber industry.

In 1869, President Ulysses S. Grant nominated Woods to the U. S. District Circuit Court. As a judge, he spent the next eleven years traveling throughout the six southern states in his district. In 1880, President Rutherford B. Hayes appointed him to the United States Supreme Court, where he served until his death in 1887.

A simple funeral was held for Woods in Washington D. C. before he was returned by train to Newark for burial. Hundreds of people lined the sidewalks as the lengthy funeral procession made its way up First Street to Trinity Episcopal Church. The Courthouse was draped in black, and businesses were closed during the funeral. Newark was in mourning.

The Reverend Paul Sterling presided over the service, conducted according to the solemn, beautiful Episcopal ritual. Chief Justice of the Supreme Court, Morrison Remick Waite, and Justice Horace Gray were in attendance, along with numerous other dignitaries. The burial service followed at Cedar Hill Cemetery.

The one time lawyer, Mayor of Newark, Speaker of the Ohio House, Civil War General, businessman, and U.S. Supreme Court Justice was now home, and at rest.

Lost on the Sultana

Dan Fleming

Excerpt of a letter from Pvt. Morris Allen to his father, Noah Allen of Clay Lick, April 5, 1865:

"Dear Father, I have once more seated myself with pen in hand to write a few lines to you to let you know that I am well and all of the boys that is with me as you might expect after laying in prison 10 months. Joseph Lease (Leese), R. Wilson, John Litle (Little), M. Wilcox, B. Vanhorn and myself have went through the Confederacy safe…We left Andersonville the 25th of March and was passed through our lines the 1st of April…We have just drew some clothing today and got cleaned up again…I tell you what we have seen hard times since the 10th of June…We are in camp four miles from Vicksburg. There is talk of us leaving here soon and it is supposed that we will be sent to Camp Chase, Ohio."

Pvt. Allen was writing from Camp Fisk, a Union camp set up for the exchange of prisoners. He had recently left Andersonville Prison in Georgia. Nineteen days later, he and some 1,800-2,000 other released P.O.W.s boarded the steamship, Sultana, along with other soldiers, civilians and crew to an unconfirmed total of about 2,400. The ship was built for a capacity of 376 people, although it could normally handle the load. They were finally returning home up the Mississippi River, over a third of them to Ohio.

Just north of Memphis in the early morning of April 27, a boiler exploded, resulting in the worst maritime disaster in U.S. history. The explosion and sinking of the boat resulted in the deaths of about 1,900 of the passengers, even more people than were lost on the Titanic. There was little news coverage of the event, because the newspapers were preoccupied with the end of the war and Lincoln's assassination on April 14.

A decent account of the tragedy cannot be made in this short space, but there are several good books about it. Morris Allen, Joseph Leese, John Little and Marvin Wilcox, all mentioned above, were killed that night, so close to going home after enduring the horrors of war and Andersonville Prison. They had all served in the 95th O.V.I., Company F.

Two others from Licking County who died that night were Charles Roberts of the 12th O.V.I., Company E, and Thomas Thomas of the 76th, Company H.

As bodies were gathered from the cold waters of the Mississippi, they were taken to Elmwood Cemetery in Memphis for burial. At a later date, they were moved to the Memphis National Cemetery. Local lore relates that as they brought out each coffin to move it, the soldier's name was printed on top in chalk. Then, before they could be reinterred, a rain storm washed away all the names—a third disaster for those hapless P.O.W.s. This cemetery has the second largest number of unknown graves of any national cemetery.

Markers for "Unknowns" at the Memphis National Cemetery.
Photo by Dan Fleming.

Licking County Survivors of the Sultana Steamship Explosion

Dan Fleming

Although there were several Licking County soldiers lost in the Sultana boiler explosion, there were some who survived.

William D. Lugenbeal served with the 135th Ohio National Guard, Company F. He had been captured at the Battle of North Mountain Depot and sent to Andersonville Prison. He survived the Sultana disaster by killing the captain's pet alligator and using its crate to float to safety. He settled in Hanover for a few years, then lived out the rest of his life as a farmer in Perryton where he is buried.

Robert Wilson and Burriss Vanhorn were in Company F of the 95th O.V.I.. They were captured on June 10, 1864 and spent ten months at Andersonville. Wilson came from Madison Township where his family owned a 65 acre farm. He survived the Sultana by jumping into the Mississippi River and holding onto something floating in the water until his rescue. After the war, he married and moved to Granville Township.

Vanhorn was born in Pennsylvania around 1827 and enlisted in Licking County on Feb. 8, 1862 as a private. He lived in Licking Township, Muskingum County after the war, and died in Indiana around 1890-92. Nothing is known of his experience during the Sultana explosion, except that he was on board.

James Stone and James W. McCarty both enlisted in January 1864 as privates in the 76th O.V.I., Co. D. Stone was born around 1841. It is believed he was from the Kirkersville area.

Grave marker for William D. Lugenbeal at Perryton Cemetery.
Photo by Dan Fleming.

Both were P.O.W.'s and were mustered out on July 15, 1865.

James Thompson was a wagoner and a private in the 76th O.V.I., Company A. Little could be found about him, except that he was aboard the Sultana and was mustered out of service on June 8, 1865.

Edward W. Evans was born around 1843. He joined Company D of the 1st Cavalry and was captured on April 1, 1865. He was aboard the Sultana, and records show that he was mustered out of service on September 20, 1865.

James Anderson was also in the 1st Cavalry, Company D, and was from Newark. He was wounded on May 30, 1862 and injured during the Sultana explosion, but he lived to be mustered out on May 20, 1865.

Albert Norris served with the 76th O.V.I., Company A in Tennessee and Georgia. He was captured at the Battle of Atlanta on October 28, 1864 and imprisoned for six months. When the boiler exploded on the Sultana, he was thrown against it, which burned his shoulder. He managed to jump overboard and floated on a cracker barrel until his rescue. Norris died in 1936 at 94 years old and was buried at Maple Grove Cemetery in Granville. He was the last known survivor of the disaster.

One other survivor was Rev. Emanuel Hush Yeisley of the 76th O.V.I., Company G, who had been a prisoner at Cahaba Prison in Alabama for six months. He was born in Amsterdam, near Jacksontown, Ohio, but his family moved to Ashland County when he was about two years old, followed by moves to Delaware County and then Van Wert County. Despite the moving, he enlisted at Jacksontown in Licking County in November 1861. He survived being scalded on the Sultana and held onto two boards in the water until his rescue. He was married later that year and became a preacher at Sugar Ridge, Ohio for 15 years before moving to Missouri. Yeisley died in 1931 at 90 years old.

I enlisted in Co. G 76 O.V.I. for three years on or about 20th of Nov. 1861 in Jackson Town Licking Co. Ohio one mile from where I was born. I served my country as a Soldier 3 years & 7 months. I was a Prisoner of War 6 months in Cahaba prison Alabama paroled March 1865 was on the Vesal Sultana that blu up Aprile 27 1865 was bad scalded discharged at Camp Chase Ohio...

[original spelling and phrasing from his own account]
– Rev. Emanuel Hush Yeisley

HEALERS

Dr. Edwin Sinnet. Photo courtesy of the Granville Historical Society.

Civil War Medicine

Peter J. D'Onofrio, Ph.D.

During the American Civil War, 1861-1865, according to Livermore,* "the Union had the equivalent of 1,556,678 three-year enlistments throughout the conflict, and the Confederacy somewhere in the vicinity of 1,083,000. No one will ever know for sure, but approximately 620,000 men perished, a figure of death that tops the total fatalities of all other wars in which Americans have fought. Of this number, 360,000 were lost to the North and 260,000 to the South." During the course of the war, the average soldier could expect to become sick 5 or 6 times. This placed a tremendous burden on the medical departments of the North and of the South.

The American Civil War took place at the end of the medical Middle Ages. Physicians were rejecting the practice of bleeding their patients to rid them of "bad humors" and of giving them heroic doses of medicines. Anesthetics such as chloroform and ether were in use by the time the war started. However, medicine practiced during this war was in the Pre-Lister era when antisepsis and asepsis were yet to be discovered by the men of medicine. It has been stated that if the Civil War had taken place between 1871 and 1875, instead of when it did, many, many thousands of young men, both North and South, would probably have survived the conflict.

We must not forget that the medical professionals of the Civil War era were some of the best trained doctors of their time, given the standards of care and knowledge that existed during the most turbulent time in American history.

Following are some of the Confederate medical advancements during the war.

1. Bean's dental fixation device

2. Smith's anterior leg splint

3. Hermetical sealing of sucking chest wounds

4. Use of indigenous plants

5. Use of plasterboard splints for mandible fractures

6. The Confederacy was the first army to make dentistry a separate field within its military.

Specific accomplishments for the North were as follows:

1. Mobile military hospitals reached a degree of development hitherto unknown.

2. Accumulation of adequate records and detailed reports for the first time permitted a complete military medical history. This led to the publication of the *Medical and Surgical History of the War of the Rebellion*, identified in Europe as the first major academic accomplishment by United States medicine.

3. Development of a system of managing mass casualties, including aid stations, field hospitals, and general hospitals, set the pattern for management of the wounded through the Vietnam War.

4. Development of the first organized ambulance corps and the first use of railroads and ships for transportation of the sick and wounded.

5. The pavilion-style general hospitals, such as Chimborazzo in Richmond and Satterlee in Philadelphia, were well-ventilated and clean, and were copied in the design of large civilian hospitals over the next 75 years, includ-

ing the Johns Hopkins Hospital in Baltimore, Maryland.

6. The importance of immediate, definitive treatment of wounds and fractures was demonstrated, and it was shown that major operative procedures, such as amputations, were optimally carried out in the first 24 hours after wounding.

7. The importance of sanitation and hygiene in preventing infection, disease, and death among the troops in the field was demonstrated.

8. Separate hospitals for smallpox, venereal disease, eye problems, nervous disorders, gangrene, etc. were established, setting a needed precedent.

9. Female nurses were introduced to hospital care and the first nurse corps was developed.

10. The Catholic orders entered the hospital business.

11. The Sanitary Commission was formed, a civilian-organized soldiers' relief society that set the pattern for the development of the American Red Cross.

12. Sanitary Fairs for raising monies for relief of the sick and wounded were established.

13. The experience and training of thousands of physicians were upgraded and they were introduced to new ideas and standards of care. These included familiarity with prevention and treatment of infectious disease, with anesthetic agents, and with surgical principles that rapidly advanced the overall quality of American medical practice.

14. The development of the Army Medical Museum, now the National Museum of Health and Medicine, a division of the Armed Forces Institute of Pathology, and the Army Medical School.

15. The staining of histopathologic slides and photomicrog-

raphy were introduced.

16. Hodgen's Splint for femur fractures.

**Numbers and Losses in the Civil War in America 1861-65*, by Thomas L. Livermore, 2002 repr.

Physicians of Licking County
During the Civil War

Dan Fleming

Licking County did not lack for medical expertise during the American Civil War. Dr. N. Cole of Etna and Dr. Thomas B. Hood of Newark were both certified by the Army Medical Board as Surgeon's Mates in October 1861. By November 6 that year, Dr. Hood was appointed Assistant Surgeon for the 76th O.V.I.. He was present at the battle at Fort Donelson, then resigned his position in January 1863. His son, T. B. Hood, Jr., also became a doctor and advertised his practice in 1861.

Dr. Edwin Sinnet was Surgeon of the 17th O.V.I., but resigned his post in March 1862 to resume his practice in Granville. He enlisted again in August 1862 in the 94th O.V.I. and found himself in charge of the hospital in Nashville, Tennessee. A letter home on February 6, 1863 described his hospital experience. In his charge were three assistant surgeons, one steward, one druggist, a ward master, 15 nurses and four cooks. He described several unusual bullet wounds and stressed the importance of surgery as soon as possible after the wound. Each wounded man was given 20-30 days furlough.

Dr. H. T. Lacy of Franklin Township was Assistant Surgeon of the 101st Ohio, and was captured at Chickamauga and sent to Libby Prison without regard for his occupation. Dr. John O. Wagstaff of Newark graduated from the Cleveland Medical College in 1860, practiced medicine in Licking County and moved to Indiana in 1862. He became Assistant Surgeon of the 54th Indiana and died of fever on January 30, 1863. A Dr. Gregory was Assistant Surgeon of Co. A, 5th OVM National Guard. Dr. Milton Henderson of Newark was Assistant Surgeon at the Cincinnati hospital in 1863. He died in Nashville in December 1864 of what was called "rheumatism at the heart."

Back home, Dr. James J. Hamill was the examining surgeon for draft exemptions, after returning from working at a hospital near Sharpsburg. In August 1862 he stated that he was unable to keep up with all the claims. He was assisted by Dr. L. T. Ballou, who was later appointed examining surgeon for pensions. After the war, Dr. Ballou developed a large clientele among the poorer folks in Newark and was greatly mourned at his death in 1874.

Dr. John N. Wilson, besides being very active in the Newark community, worked on a committee to aid sick and wounded soldiers who came through town at the Newark Depot. He recruited for the 76th Regiment and handled distribution of paychecks to them. Finally, a Dr. Rissler was the first president of the Hebron Medical Society in July 1862.

Dr. Edwin Sinnet

Theresa Overholser and Margaret Brooks

Authors and historians like nothing better than the first hand observations found in letters written by famous leaders during times of national crisis. These letters give insights into events and decisions that might have affected world history. At the other end of the spectrum, "ordinary" servicemen and women have always written letters to their loved ones at home. Eagerly awaited, read and reread, passed down to children and grandchildren, these letters become treasured family heirlooms and eventually valued historical documents. The Granville Historical Society is fortunate to have a collection of letters written between a young couple separated during the American Civil War that are of special interest during this year's sesquicentennial commemoration.

Dr. Edwin Sinnet of Granville, Ohio joined the 17th Ohio Volunteer Infantry as a surgeon in the late summer of 1861. He resigned that post in March 1862 to resume his practice in Granville, but reenlisted in August 1862 as a surgeon with the 94th O.V.I. His young wife, Sarah Wright Sinnet, was left at home with their two-year old daughter, Alice. Their letters to one another touch on worries and problems that still are universal whenever a couple must be parted by duty.

Each worried about the health and safety of the other, while minimizing the fears they faced themselves. Edwin made light of the dangers around him, telling Sarah that the reports of the war she read in the newspaper were exaggerated and that the writers turned short skirmishes into battles with many casualties. Sarah became dangerously ill but gave

Edwin only the briefest description of her symptoms. After receiving letters and telegrams from Sarah's family, Edwin took leave to be with her until she was better. Both fussed over Alice, always hoping that she would recover quickly from her colds and sore throats, well aware of the limits of 1860s medical care in fighting infection.

Money worries seem to have surprised the couple. Instead of a steady income of cash, iou's, and work traded for medical care, the Sinnets suddenly found themselves "without a copper cent," as Sarah put it. Edwin advised her to go over the books and find someone owing them who might be able to pay in cash. Of course Sarah hesitated, never before having had to engage in business affairs. So she asked her brother to see to collecting for her. After several months without pay, Edwin was finally able to send home more than Sarah needed to keep the household running. Then the problem became what to do with the excess. Edwin advised her not to put it in the bank, but rather to find someone they trusted who would borrow it from her at a good rate of interest.

Although neither ever voiced it in their letters, certainly there was a longing to take the other's place for a while, or at least to experience life through their eyes. Edwin was running a hospital, learning new surgical skills, dining with the officers, and spending some leisure time exploring the countryside around camp. He sent home interesting plants, minerals and fossils, even a puppy for little Alice. Sarah, meanwhile, was in the midst of beloved family and friends, enjoying watching Alice grow and learn. She helped decorate the new Presbyterian Church building, and saw her first Christmas tree.

A new baby girl arrived shortly after Edwin reenlisted for a second tour of duty. Sarah teased him by never giving the child the same name twice—Amanda, Nellie, Nettie, or just "baby." She would be christened Clara after her father finally was able to hold her.

Dr. Sinnet returned from the war and became a very successful businessman. He was involved in banking, politics, and manufacturing as well as medicine. Baby Clara grew up to be a great benefactor to Granville, eventually entrusting her parents' Civil War correspondence to the Granville Historical Society.

Note: This story was partially written as a promotional article for a program at the Bryn Du Mansion on October 20, 2011, sponsored by the Granville Historical Society and the Bryn Du Commission, featuring period music, displays and a lecture about Civil War surgery. Excerpts from the letters of Dr. Sinnet and his wife were read by people portraying them.

Newark Avenue Named After Veteran of Army of Northern Virginia

Doug Stout

Y ou may be surprised to learn that an avenue in Newark was actually named for a veteran of the Confederacy. Henry Day was 21 and living in Warrentown, Virginia when the war started. He enrolled as a private on April 22, 1861 in the 17th Virginia Infantry, Company K, also known as the "Warrenton Rifles."

He was not the only Day to enlist; his brother, Dr. Douglas Day, who had a practice in Zanesville, enlisted as a surgeon in the 22nd Ohio Volunteer Infantry until their sister heard about it and wrote the doctor on May 22, 1861. Her letter said in part, "We were surprised and grieved to see by a paper which was received, the announcement of your appointment as surgeon in one of the Ohio regiments. It cannot be that you are leagued with those miserable abolitionists who thirst for our blood & will never be satisfied unless they obtain it." Her postscript said, "God grant that you may choose the right side, which is ours, & she must prevail." Douglas resigned his commission on July 5, 1861. One can only assume it was because of the letter from Jennie, who also told him that Henry had enlisted and, "if you join the Northern army you will never be able to come here again with any satisfaction." So ended his military career.

Henry, with the 17th Virginia, was eventually assigned to General George Pickett's division. He and the 17th took part in First and Second Manassas, and the Peninsula Campaign in which his younger brother, Alex, also of company K, died of disease in Richmond. They were at Antietam, Fredericksburg, Bermuda Hundred, Five Forks and Salyers Creek, where he was captured on April 6, 1865 by troops led by Somerset's General Philip Sheridan. Lee's army surrendered on April 9, 1865. Ironically, the 17th had been sent to defend Richmond instead of marching to Gettysburg, the battle that Pickett's name is best known for. What a sad reunion that would have been when the 17th rejoined what was left of Pickett's division.

Henry enrolled in medical school after the war, following in his father's and brother's footsteps, and received his degrees from the University of Virginia and University of Maryland in 1868. The economy was not the best in the South in 1868. Since Henry's brother, Douglas, was still in Zanesville, he moved north to Licking County to set up practice. He married Mary Robinson of Gratiot in 1871. They purchased two lots in Brownsville in 1873 and in 1875 bought a farm in Avondale at Buckeye Lake. They also lived in Jacksontown as Henry's practice grew. They later moved to Newark.

In a letter to his sister Eliza in Virginia, dated Oct. 15, 1902, Henry wrote, "We are getting in shape to turn a part of our eight acres here into town lots. Newark is extending out our way and beyond us. Our lots becoming more valuable every year, all (its) attractions here are out our way." On August 9, 1905 the 24 lots of the Day Addition were added to the City of Newark. These lots made up what would be the east side of Day Avenue and were behind Dr. Day's house, which was on the corner of what is now W. Main and Day Avenue.

Henry served Newark as health official for six years and physician at the county infirmary for nine years, while still keeping his private practice at 6 ½ W. Main Street.

He made a new home in the North, but that does not mean

Dr. Henry Day.
From *Photographic History of Newark and Licking County*, 1904.

he had forgotten his past. In the same letter quoted above he thanked his sister for sending a clipping from a local newspaper about the exploits of the Warrenton Rifles at Fairfax C.H. during the war and also told her that he had received and filled out his application for "the Corps of Honor."

Henry passed away at his home on July 30, 1918 at the age of 79 and was buried outside Jacksontown in Fairmont Cemetery. In 1992 a Confederate marker was placed on his grave to remember his service to the Confederacy. Was the rebel reconstructed with his northern neighbors? His obituary dated July 31, 1918 reads: "It was characteristic of him that he gave unbounded charity and was never known to press the poor for payment of a bill." Henry's life shows that after four years of suffering, death and carnage, he and countless veterans like him on both sides learned that enemies can put aside their differences and work together to make a stronger and truly United States of America.

Some of the ladies of Charleston are untiring in their efforts to contribute to the comfort of our sick soldiers.

– Erasmus White, in *Newark Advocate*, Nov. 8, 1861

REMEMBERING

Reunion of the veterans of the 76th O.V.I., at the Great Circle Mound in Newark, Ohio, July 22, 1890. From the collection of Ronna Eagle.

Soldiers' Relief Committee

Dan Fleming

Due to the railroads passing through Newark, sick and wounded soldiers often stopped off at the Newark Depot to wait for other trains to take them home. They often did not have money to put themselves up somewhere or buy meals. Even many returning Licking County soldiers often had to tarry in Newark for a while before they could go home. This happened much more frequently by spring of 1862, a year after the war began. A few leaders in Newark saw the need to find a way to help them.

On May 3, 1862, Lucius Case chaired a meeting at the court house to solve this problem. He had been one of the men who helped frame the 1851 version of the Ohio Constitution. A notice in the *Newark Advocate* stated, "It is not a very pleasant thing for men who were cheered and feasted when on their way to the battle field, to find themselves deserted and uncared for on their return." At the meeting, a committee was formed to solicit funding wherever possible. The committee consisted of Isaac Smucker, who had written the resolutions for the group, W. L. Hager, Dr. John N. Wilson, A. W. Dennis, Thomas J. Davis, David Moore, Thomas J. Anderson and Lucius Case.

They were successful in making arrangements with township trustees to raise the needed money to get the project started. Peter Smith's home was hired out as lodging since it was located near the station. They spent $21.25 at the outset to help 35 returning soldiers, but there was no more available money in the township treasury beyond that. The committee next appealed to all citizens with the help of the ladies of the Soldiers' Aid Society. By October, they had spent a total of $63.77 to attend to almost 200 soldiers. They screened each case carefully to determine if it was legitimate.

In January 1863, the committee publicly thanked the Second Presbyterian Church for money raised among its congregation. There were likely many other churches that contributed, but we do not have a record of them. In fact, this was the last mention we could find in the *Advocate* of the Soldiers' Relief Committee. As the war dragged on, higher numbers of soldiers returned wounded or ill. It could be that there was simply not enough money left within Licking County's families to continue the effort after more and more men enlisted or were drafted each year.

Grand Army of the Republic Posts of Licking County, Ohio

Larry Stevens

The Grand Army of the Republic (G.A.R.) was the largest Union veteran's organization in the United States after the Civil War. It was based upon three objectives: fraternity, charity and loyalty. The fraternal ideal was encouraged by having regular meetings of local posts, state encampments and national meetings. Local posts set up charitable funds for needy veterans, widows and orphans and promoted soldiers' and orphans' homes. The veteran "Boys in Blue" spent much of their time promoting loyalty by encouraging the preservation of Civil War sites, relics and historic documents. Another project was soliciting funds for monuments and memorials, busts and equestrian statues of Union soldiers and heroes.

The G.A.R. became politically active and powerful. Having such a large membership allowed the old soldiers to sway many votes and laws their way. Between the years 1868 and 1908, no Republicans were nominated to the United States Presidency without an endorsement from the G.A.R.

Decoration Day was first celebrated by the G.A.R. when it requested members of all posts to decorate the graves of their fallen comrades with flowers on May 30, 1868. This has over the years changed into the present Memorial Day Holiday.

Nine G.A.R. posts and one Woman's Relief Corps were located within Licking County. Posts were named after heroic figures who made great sacrifices during the Civil War.

A brief history of each post follows:

Lemert Post 71, Newark.

Chartered May 14, 1881 and named for Thaddeus Lemert, Captain of Co. A, 76th Ohio Volunteer Infantry. Lemert met death with true heroism. Realizing his fate he said, "Our forefathers died for their country, why should not I?" He died January 11th, 1863 leading a charge on the works at Arkansas Post, Arkansas.

The charter members of the Post were: James W. Owens, W.C. Lyon, George W. Chase, A.E. Magoffin, James R. Kingston, Dr. J. Wotring, Rev. John Tenney, James M. Browne, H.P. Courtier, Dr. F.O. Jacobs, George M. Williams, Charles C. Rankin, Edward F. Newkirk, Nelson M. Lamb, Edward F. Cross, Joseph C. Wehrle, Wm. H. O'Bannon, J.W. Lattimer, Fred H. Wilson, George A. Ball, Loyal H. Clouse, George H. Boggs, Chas. D. Miller, J.B. Vance, Ezra McConnell, Michael S. Finegan, David J. Jones, Ezra H. Smith, Franklin Wise, Nathan Bostwick and Thomas Cochran.

Channel Post 188, Utica.

Chartered January 14, 1882 and named for Aaron Channel, Captain of Co. E, 12th Ohio Volunteer Infantry. He was mortally wounded on the 9th day of May 1864, at the battle of Cloyd's Mountain, Virginia.

The charter members of the Post were: Jesse Wilson, David A. Sinsabaugh, W.T. O'Bannon, D.P. Campbell, H. Bricker, Levi Knowlton, Wm. L. Belt, C.E. Dering, J.L. Van Allen, Wilson White, W.F. Smoots, John Worrell, James Blazer, David McClelland and Henry Bash.

Hamilton Post 311, Gratiot.

Chartered April 6, 1883 and was named for three sons of Robert and Mary Hamilton of Brownsville, Ohio and one son of William and Marian Hamilton. The three brothers were: (1st) William M. Hamilton, Co. B, 135th Ohio Volunteer Infantry. He was taken prisoner near Winchester, Virginia in the summer of 1864 and exchanged eight months later in horrendous condition. William died at Annapolis, Maryland on January 3, 1865 at 26 years of age. (2nd) Captain Arthur T. Hamilton, Adjutant of the 9th Ohio Volunteer Cavalry, was mortally wounded at Aiken, South Carolina and died at Cheraw, South Carolina on March 6th, 1865 at 22 years of age. (3rd) Henry Hamilton, Musician, Co. G, 32nd Ohio Volunteer Infantry, died of camp fever at Beverly, West Virginia, December 12, 1861 at 21 years of age. (4th) Robert J. Hamilton, cousin of the other three, Musician, Co. G, 32nd Ohio Volunteer Infantry was mortally wounded at Camp Alleghany, West Virginia, December 13, 1861. He died at Zanesville, Ohio, December 28, 1861 at 19 years of age.

Original officers of the Post were: P.C., Warner Mills; S.V.C., William Tucker; J.V.C., C.A. Cook; Adjt., J.H. Bell; Q.M., E.R. Standiford; O.D., T.B. Iden; O.G., William Hazlett; Chaplain, Thomas Caldwell; Surg., A.D.S. McArthur; S.M., W.S. McMaster and Q.M.S., Lewis Buckingham.

Josia Baird Post 653, Pataskala.

Chartered October 22, 1883 and named for Pvt. Josia Baird who enlisted at Pataskala and entered the service in Co. D of the 13th Missouri Volunteer Infantry, which later became the 22nd Ohio Volunteer Infantry. Josia was in the battles of Fort Donelson, Shiloh and Corinth. He was ambushed and killed by guerilla gunfire while with a volunteer forage party near Brownsville, Arkansas on July 20, 1864.

The charter members of the Post were: I.N. Milburn, John Laughery, B.F. Sutherland, Martin Slough, G.A. Clifton, David Headley, Ira Lyons, S.A. Dulan, F.B. Elliott, Wm. King, Geo. Spelman, Albert Pugh, Alden Besse, Joseph Atkinson,

Charles Stewart, Wm. W. McMillen, Wm. Lemmon, Abraham Fast, J.H. Baird, C.R. Langdon, W.C. Green, Thomas Lennington and W.H. Gardner.

T. and J. Dill Post 463, Homer.

Chartered June 20, 1884 and named for Knox County brothers Thomas M. Dill and John A. Dill. They enlisted at Homer in the autumn of 1861 entering Co. H, 76th Ohio Volunteer Infantry. Thomas, a Sergeant, was wounded with a spent ball at Fort Donelson, Tennessee and furloughed home. He died of complications at a hospital in St. Louis, Missouri on March 23, 1863. John, a 1st Lieutenant, was captured a few days after the battle of Shiloh. He became sick and died at a private residence near Corinth, Mississippi.

The charter members of the Post were: R.S. Fulton, J.P. Fletcher, J.R. Looker, J.H. Glaze, Morgan Beever, Adam Williams, Mervin Buxton, Henry N. Tippett, John H. Day, David Hunter, Joseph S. Murphy, R.W. Larimore, Harvey Simmons, Samuel Yoakam, E.E. Lockwood, David Weaver, Wm. H. Robinson, Wm. Chapman and Wm. Rockwell.

Z.P. Evans Post 668, Perryton.

Charter date unknown. Named for Zebulon P. Evans who entered service as a Sergeant and was promoted to Captain of Co. A, 76th Ohio Volunteer Infantry. He was one of the best officers of the regiment and had the love and the confidence of his men. Evans mustered out at the end of the war with Co. A. and died a few years later.

Ira P. French Post 693, Johnstown.

Charter date unknown. Named for Ira P. French Co. B, 76th Ohio Volunteer Infantry. He mustered in as a 1st Lieutenant and was promoted to Captain. French was killed leading his men in battle at Ringgold, Georgia on November 27th, 1863.

J.L. Francis Post 704, St. Louisville.

Charter date unknown. Named for Captain John L. Francis, Co. F, 135th Ohio Volunteer Infantry (National Guard). Captured at North Mountain Depot, West Virginia, July 3rd, 1864. He died in Columbia Prison, Columbia, South Carolina on December 6th, 1864 at 24 years old.

Garfield Post 749, Jersey.

Charter date unknown. Named for Colonel James A. Garfield, 42nd Ohio Volunteer Infantry (later President of the United States).

Woman's Relief Corps, No. 45.
Auxiliary of Lemert Post 71, Newark.

Chartered on June 13th, 1884. The charter members of the Corps were: Emely J. Lamb, Sarah J. Huston, Sarah Armstrong, Annie Wright, Ella Ashbrook, Sarah C. Bourner, Helen Naylor, Louisa Miller, Ellen Vandergriff, Mary Peckham, Hester McCrum, Annie Wiley, Emeline Haughey, Martha Cady, Ida Swartz, Carrie Hillborn, Romie Soliday, Victoria Clark, Maggie Stafford, Mary Marsh, Martha Crawford, Maggie Conley, Mary Francis and Elizabeth McManus.

Hattie E. Dew

Dan Fleming

Women of Licking County played a vital role during the Civil War. They formed the Soldiers' Aid Society and collected food, clothing and medical supplies to send to the field. They sewed regimental flags. They made quilts to raise money for the war effort and to comfort soldiers. They voiced their attitudes about abolition.

One woman who deserves more recognition was Harriet (Hattie) E. Dew. She was born in Rushville, Ohio on December 2, 1837, daughter of William and Sarah Wilson. She married A. O. Beckwith in Fairfield County in 1855. Beckwith had previously lived in Licking County. When the Civil War began, he joined the 63rd Ohio Volunteer Infantry, serving as quartermaster. He died on May 16, 1863. Thus, Hattie lost her first husband to the war. Their only child, Harry, died at 7 years old.

Hattie married Elias Dew in 1873 in Zanesville. He was a widower, giving Hattie four step-children. He was born into a Quaker family in 1825 in Jefferson County. In 1855 he began working for the Central Ohio Railroad out of Bellaire and Cambridge, until he moved to North Carolina in January 1861. He was an engineer there on several routes until he relocated to Florida in February 1862. He must have been aiding the South through his job during this time. In Florida, he worked for the railroad for six months and then signed up for an ocean steamer called the "Mayflower" to run a blockade to Cuba. He was captured by Union forces, imprisoned at Key West, and then paroled. He made his way back to Ohio by March 1863 and worked again for the Central Ohio Railroad. His job moved him around many times, but he was in Newark by 1871 when the B. & O. first moved its headquarters there. He was a charter member of the Brotherhood of Locomotive Engineers, and was present when the first mail run by train was made from Newark to Granville. Elias died in 1906.

Hattie E. Dew. From the collection of the Licking County Historical Society. This photograph was originally placed into the cornerstone of the Soldiers and Sailors Memorial Building.

Imagine the stories Hattie must have heard from both sides of the war through both husbands. On January 28, 1891, while attending a meeting of the G.A.R. Auxiliary called Sheridan Circle #6, Hattie proposed that the community erect a building in memory of its veterans. It would be called the Soldiers and Sailors Memorial. A public meeting was held on February 23, presided over by Judge E. M. P. Brister, where the idea was very popular. An act was passed by the Ohio Legislature on April 9 approving the building, and a board of trustees was appointed. A local bond levy passed to raise money for it.

By June 1894, the building was ready for the cornerstone to be laid, and a huge ceremony took place. In the cornerstone, among current newspapers, military rosters and other memorabilia were placed photographs of Major David A. B. Moore, Capt. Leonidas McDougal, and Hattie E. Dew. The contents of the cornerstone now reside at the Licking County Historical Society.

Soldiers & Sailors Memorial Building

Dan Fleming

On January 28, 1891, Hattie E. Dew proposed to the Sheridan Circle #6 (a women's auxiliary of the G.A.R.) that the community erect a building in memory of its veterans. That group's resolutions were read at a regular G.A.R. meeting, which resulted in the Licking County Soldiers' Memorial Association. The idea was very well received, so a public meeting was held at the court house on February 23 to get community reaction. Judge E. M. P. Brister presided.

On April 9 the same year, the Association convinced the Ohio legislature to approve a bond levy to raise money to purchase a site and construct the building. Common Pleas court appointed a board of trustees, and the bond levy passed.

June 14, 1894 was a great day in Newark. First a long parade was led by Grand Marshal Lt. John H. McCune. Then the crowd of thousands converged upon the site of the newly laid foundation to witness the cornerstone ceremonies conducted by the Lemert Post #71 of the G.A.R. Governor McKinley was scheduled to be present, but had to cancel due to a scheduling conflict. Captain J. B. Vance placed a time capsule into the cornerstone with the wish "that it may remain undisturbed in its resting place so long as the union of the States shall endure." He then read off the items in the box and consecrated it with "corn as an emblem of plenty," "wine as an emblem of joy and gladness," and "oil as an emblem of peace." Then Newark Mayor Waldo Taylor addressed the group, followed by several others. The Pugh Vidette Band and the Buckeye Band played patriotic music.

The Soldiers and Sailors Memorial Building in downtown Newark, Ohio.
From Brister, *Centennial History,* 1909.

Interior of the G.A.R. Hall, Newark, Ohio. From the collection of Larry
Stevens.

The building was completed in early 1895, and the dedication ceremony was held on March 13, 1895, once again conducted by Lemert Post #71. All the old veterans attended with families and friends. Colonel Charles H. Kibler's address included an almost complete history of all the companies that left Licking County in the war. Judge S. M. Hunter spoke of the role of our women. There was a supper, recitations and music.

The building eventually included offices for the G.A.R., the Soldiers and Sailors Relief Commission, the American Legion Post 85, a museum for the Civil War and World War I, a library, meeting rooms and an opera house which came to be known as the Auditorium Theater. The Memorial Hall on the third floor was used for G.A.R. meetings with a capacity of 1,400.

The Auditorium Theater itself had a long, successful history, drawing major entertainers from around the country. Its stage was the second largest in Ohio at the time. But catastrophe struck on April 28, 1968 when an arsonist broke in and set fire to papers on a desk. The fire spread, causing the roof to collapse onto the third floor, which collapsed onto the second floor. Virtually everything was lost except the theater, which continued in use after receiving a new façade.

The building fell into disrepair, and years of fundraising efforts failed to save it. After changing hand several times, the 107-year-old Soldiers and Sailors Memorial Building was demolished in 2002. Its cornerstone was saved and presented to the Licking County Historical Society.

Civil War Veterans' Reunions

Dan Fleming

Remembering our veterans became a high priority nationwide at the end of the Civil War. Veterans wanting to share their experiences formed many types of groups.

Largest was the Grand Army of the Republic (G.A.R.), which began in Decatur, Illinois in 1866. It reached a peak membership of 400,000 by 1890. The nine Licking County chapters were formed between 1881-1884. It was a fraternal organization which held considerable political clout for elections and lobbying causes, founded on the principles of "Fraternity, Charity and Loyalty." The G.A.R. dissolved nationally in 1956.

It was the G.A.R. that first officially proclaimed the Memorial Day holiday (originally Decoration Day) on May 5, 1868, although many from North and South had already been decorating graves of soldiers. Newark's first Memorial Day celebration coincided with the first reunion of the 76th Ohio Volunteer Infantry on May 30, 1878. That was a truly grand event, attended by President Hayes and Generals Garfield, Sherman and Warner. It was thoroughly documented in a book by Major Charles D. Miller in 1878.

The 76th O.V.I. continued its annual reunions at least through 1932, when General John L. Clem travelled from Texas to attend. He was listed as the youngest member at 81, while W. A. Parr was the oldest at 96. Also in attendance were Frank French (last living survivor of the Civil War in Licking County) and Albert Norris (last living survivor of the Sultana steamship disaster).

1st Cavalry Reunion at the Licking County Courthouse, date unknown.
From the collection of Ronna Eagle.

Another notable reunion of the 76th was in 1916 when the survivors of the 1st Arkansas Regiment ceremoniously returned the regimental flag of the 76th which they had captured at the Battle of Ringgold.

The 31st O.V.I. held annual reunions at Hebron at least through 1906 when 86 veterans attended. Documentation of further meetings is difficult to find, as it is for many other groups.

The 113th O.V.I. regiment held a reunion at the Memorial Building in Newark on September 17, 1897. It contained many boys from Granville.

The 3rd O.V.I. (Captain Leonidas McDougal commanded Company H), held annual reunions through at least 1911, although the one that year was held in Columbus.

The Union Veteran Legion was another organization of Union veterans, but a bit more exclusive than the G.A.R. It was founded in Pittsburgh in 1884 for those who had served at least three years, or had been wounded and served at least

76th O.V.I. Reunion at the Licking County Courthouse, 1916.
From the collection of Ronna Eagle.

The Buckeye Band entertained at many Civil War reunions.
From the collection of Ronna Eagle.

Ribbon from the 76th O.V.I. Reunion, 1916. From the collection of Larry Stevens.

Ribbon from No. 31 U.V.L. Encampment at Newark, Ohio, date unknown. From the collection of Larry Stevens.

two years. General John H. Short of the U.V.L. visited the Lemert Post of the G.A.R. in 1889 to make arrangements for a national reunion in Newark.

There was another local veterans organization called the Soldiers and Sailors of Licking County which held annual reunions from 1885 through at least 1916. Most of them were held at Wickham's Grove in Toboso. The crowd numbered from 6,000 in 1900, steadily increasing to about 10,000 in 1910. Toboso was an interurban stop, which made it convenient for folks everywhere to ride out and back for the day. By 1916, the event was held at Baughman Park, just over the county line in Muskingum County on State Route 586. There were 3,000 visitors for the 1916 reunion.

As time wore on and more veterans died, more counties merged for their events. The 1916 reunion at Baughman Park included Licking, Muskingum, Coshocton and Fairfield Counties. All of these veterans groups and reunions faded away as the old soldiers died. The G.A.R. was taken over by the Sons of Union Veterans of the Civil War.

Ribbon presented to Major General John L. Clem at the 67th Annual Encampment of the G.A.R. in Newark, Ohio, 1933. From the collection of Marilyn Norris, passed down to her husband, Richard Norris from his great-grandfather, Frederick David Cummins, whose father was in the Civil War.

Ribbon from the State Veteran Reunion, Newark, Ohio, July 22, 1878. From the collection of Larry Stevens.

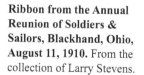

Ribbon from the Annual Reunion of Soldiers & Sailors, Blackhand, Ohio, August 11, 1910. From the collection of Larry Stevens.

The Civil War and Genealogy Research

Vera Bagent

July 1865. A four-year-old enters the kitchen. She sees her mother in the arms of a tall, bearded, dirty and dusty man wearing a wrinkled and soiled blue uniform. He is holding a long grimy rifle in one hand. He turns and sees his daughter for the first time in each of their lives, and smiles at the little tot. She lets out a scream of horror as she runs from the room. Welcome home from the war, Dad!

This event is part of the actual family lore of Vera Bagent. Ira Blanchard Holman was an aide de camp to General Grover of the 14th New Hampshire Volunteer Infantry. In researching this unit through genealogical methods, we can find much more history on the 14th NHVI and on Ira B. Holman.

Another story: The Civil War ends and the soldiers of the 76th Ohio Volunteer Infantry are mustered out. Many who had been prisoners in the South eagerly board the steamboat, Sultana, at Vicksburg, Mississippi, which is headed for its home port of St. Louis. It would stop at Cairo, Illinois to disembark the Ohio men, where they would catch a train for Columbus. Several miles up river on April 27, 1865 the steamboat explodes and thousands of Civil War veterans are severely wounded, killed and/or drowned in the cold water of the Mississippi River. The Sultana was built to hold 376 passengers, but that day there were over 2,500 on board.

On researching the life of Albert Norris, ancestor of the husband of Marilyn Norris (member of LCGS), vast amounts of information besides his family lineage came forward. He

130

was aboard the ill-fated Sultana. The boat had stopped in Vicksburg to fix a faulty boiler. The captain determined that putting in a new boiler would require too much time, and time was money. The boiler was merely patched, and the Sultana went on her way. Around Memphis, the boiler exploded, throwing hot metal and hot water into the air along with many of the passengers. It ignited the other two boilers, which exploded to sink the Sultana. Family lore told only of the relative being on board the steamboat that exploded, but further genealogical research found the missing details to make the story touch the hearts of his descendants. Norris turned out to be the last living survivor of that disaster by the time he died.

A third story tells of a Civil War soldier who was mustered out of the Union Army in Missouri and how he "forgot" to go home to his wife and three children. Instead, he went west and established himself in Arizona. Curly Bill Brocius became "Arizona's most famous outlaw." Before he joined the Union Army, he was a poor dirt farmer from Crawfordville, Indiana. Originally, he was from Licking County, Ohio and was another ancestor of Marilyn Norris. Through careful research, it was discovered that he returned to Crawfordville some years later and found his wife had remarried. He left town an angry and bitter man. From that time forward, he returned to his unlawful ways around Tombstone, Arizona. He killed men for no apparent reason. He joined the Ike Clanton Clan and spread fear throughout the region. Wyatt Earp, Sheriff of Tombstone, eventually killed Curly Bill, but not before he had become a legend. There are many legends relating to Curly Bill Brocius, some true and some folklore. A little genealogical research found this family lore to be true.

The Licking County Genealogical Society stands ready and able to help you find your ancestors. It is free and open to the public on the 2nd floor of the Licking County Library, Tuesday through Saturday, 1:00-4:00 p.m.

Civil War Medal of Honor Recipients from Licking County

Dan Fleming

We read about Lieut. Leonidas H. Inscho receiving the Medal of Honor for capturing a Confederate Captain and four of his men at the Battle of South Mountain. He was the first from Licking County to receive this high award, but there were others.

Delano J. Morey was born in Licking County in 1845, but his family moved to Delaware County by 1850 and then to Hardin County by 1860. He enlisted in the 82nd Ohio Volunteer Infantry, Co. B in February 1861 in Hardin County. During his first battle experience in Virginia, he and a group of about 150 soldiers were ordered to fix bayonets and charge down the mountain, not knowing they were approaching 4,000 Confederates. During their retreat back up, Morey pulled off to the side to capture two rebels nearby with his empty gun. He led them back to his captain. Morey was 16 years old. He returned to Hardin County after the war and became a storekeeper and farmer in later life. He died April 24, 1911 and was buried at Grove Cemetery in Kenton, Ohio.

Milton Hanna was born in 1842 in Licking County to James and Nancy Hanna. When Milton was eleven, the family moved to Minnesota. He enlisted there in June 1861 into the 2nd Minnesota Infantry, Company H. He fought at Mills Springs in Kentucky, then Shiloh, Corinth, Perryville, Stone River, Shelbyville, Tullahoma and Chickamauga. On February 15, 1863, he and 14 others were foraging in the woods when they were attacked by 125 mounted rebels from the 6th Alabama. Somehow, the Union men won this fight, driving them off and capturing three prisoners and three horses. Eight of this group were awarded the Medal of Honor. Hanna re-enlisted in December 1863 and participated in the Atlanta Campaign and Sherman's "March to the Sea." He returned to Minnesota after the war, where he became a successful businessman. He was very active in his community, especially the fire department. He died on January 21, 1913 and was buried in Glenwood Cemetery in Mankato, Minnesota.

John S. Shellenberger was born in Pennsylvania in 1839, son of David Shellenberger. He enlisted as a Corporal into the 85th Regiment of Pennsylvania Volunteers, Company B on November 12, 1861. He was awarded the Medal of Honor for capturing a Confederate flag at Deep Run, Virginia on August 16, 1864. By 1900, Shellenberger was farming for Simon Jones in Granville, Ohio. He died January 16, 1911 and was buried at Welsh Hills Cemetery in Granville.

Civil War Leads to Memorial Day
and Honors for Johnny Clem

Linda A. Leffel

*"The nation which fails to honor its heroes, the memory
of its heroes, whether those heroes be living or dead,
does not deserve to live, and will not live."*

- Hugh Gordon Miller in a speech honoring Lincoln.

Memorial Day, first known as "Decoration Day," was originally a day of remembrance for those who died in service during the tragic American Civil War. It was first proclaimed in May 1868 by General John Logan, national commander of the Grand Army of the Republic, when flowers were placed on graves of Union and Confederate soldiers at Arlington National Cemetery. Today's holiday evolved to honor those who died in battle, or served in our military, and even includes remembering non-military deceased loved ones.

Many stories surround the holiday's beginning, with various towns claiming to be the birthplace of Memorial Day. Individuals and communities exhibited a common need to honor those who sacrificed so much during the Civil War. Records show that Southern women's groups decorated graves, as did Northern citizens, even before the war's end. In 1882 it became "Memorial Day" and soldiers who had died in previous wars were also honored. It was designated a public federal holiday by 1967. In 1971 it became a "Monday Holiday," held on the last Monday of May.

Each year the Licking County Historical Society celebrates the life of Civil War hero, John Clem. Why honor Johnny? He represents countless boys determined to join the fight. It is estimated that over 10,000 boys under age 18 enlisted on the Union side (Southern records are more uncertain)--some as young as Johnny (just under 10). These boys performed dangerous, but important duties as drummers communicating orders, couriers, regular soldiers, or carrying out camp chores.

Controversy about Johnny exists, as his exploits are not easily verified. In the Disney movie *Johnny Shiloh*, and the book of the same name, plus numerous articles, he was depicted as a hero at the Battle of Shiloh, which now seems impossible. After heroic actions at battles like Chickamauga, Johnny became somewhat of a national celebrity when presented that the youngster had been wounded, taken prisoner, and had even shot a Confederate officer off his horse. But stories were not always accurate, which serves as an obstacle to his historic record.

In 1989 Civil War researcher, Greg Pavelka, disputed Johnny's record. This led to the Blue and Gray Central Ohio Civil War Roundtable protecting Johnny's honor with a "mock trial" held in our historic Court House. John Clem Elementary student, James Galbraith, proudly defended Johnny's deeds by portraying him. In 1999, local veterans commissioned a permanent statue to honor Johnny; a bust-replica for his school namesake was also presented. More recent writings, and documentary movie *Johnny* premiering here in 2007, have tried to give a more accurate view of Johnny's honorable career.

We again honor Johnny Clem this year on Saturday, May 21st with people dressed in period costume, Civil War era music, a delicious breakfast, John Clem displays, Clem Elementary students singing, and of course students portraying Johnny and his sister, Lizzie! A morning of friends, food and fun... we think Johnny would be proud!

Note: This story served partially as a promotion for the annual "John Clem Memorial Breakfast" at the Buckingham House on May 21, 2011, sponsored by the Licking County Historical Society.

Echoes of the Civil War
Found at Cedar Hill Cemetery

Linda A. Leffel and Emily Larson

Y ou can find the impact of the Civil War on our community by walking through grave markers at Cedar Hill Cemetery. Glance at names and dates on tombstones—there you can find personal stories of men who gave so much during this difficult time, and those who waited diligently at home. The Licking County Historical Society loves connecting you with stories of past citizens each year at our Annual Graveyard Walk. The event on September 9, 2011 featured the following people:

Two Newark brothers were among those young men who went to war in 1861: William and Charles Woods. William was already an honored Yale graduate admitted to the Ohio Bar by the time he was appointed Lt. Col. of the 76th Ohio Volunteer Infantry in 1861, serving under his younger brother, Charles R. Woods. William achieved the rank of brevet major general and endured many battles, including being part of Sherman's "March to the Sea" campaign. After the war, his new home was Alabama rather than Ohio. Among his accomplishments was being appointed to the U.S. Supreme Court by President Rutherford B. Hayes. Charles Woods had graduated from West Point in 1852 and became a career officer. With his promotion to Colonel, he was given command of the 76th Ohio and was with his brother in Sherman's "March to the Sea." He remained in the army after the war, achieving the rank of brevet brigadier general. When retired from military service, he returned to Newark to his estate "Woodside," at the site of what is now the former Woodside School on Woods Avenue.

Surgeon Dr. James Black was practicing in Hebron when the war began. He joined the 113th O.V.I. and accomplished valuable work during the war, from serving as brigade medical director to organizing hospital service through the army of Tennessee. Upon returning to Newark, he became a very talented and well-known writer on various medical topics.

Successful businessman Brevet Major Charles D. Miller had lived in Newark only a few years when he enlisted, assigned as a recruiter. Later with the 76th O.V.I., he survived wounds during many battles in his three years of service. Eventually the businessman would retire to Florida, returning to Newark at the end of his life.

Captain John and Eleanor McCune were involved and prominent community members. Their beautiful home still stands at the corner of Church and 2nd Streets. John dedicated three years to Company H of the 31st Ohio Volunteer Infantry, leading men in such battles as Chickamauga. Even with later financial problems, the family continued to prosper in the hardware business.

Eliza Johnson has stories to share through letters which give us a glimpse of what people were feeling during these difficult years. Not only did her husband serve for a short time, her half- brother Theodore also joined, but with the Confederates. Letters written between them describe a painful time when he was a prisoner of war. He would eventually come home to his sister and raise a family in Newark.

Previously highlighted at one of our events was Leonidas Inscho, honored for being the first Licking Countian awarded the Medal of Honor. His medal is in the collection of the Licking County Historical Society at the Sherwood Davidson House. Leonidas remained an involved community member throughout his life, even being commandant of the military training grounds at the Octagon Mound.

Note: This story served as a promotion for the annual Cedar Hill Cemetery Walk on September 9, 2011, sponsored by the Licking County Historical Society, and performed by the Licking County Players Suitcase Theater Group. The event in 2011 was called "Echoes from the Past" and featured seven Civil War soldiers.

The Works, Central to 150th Civil War Commemoration

Janice LoRaso

Introductory Paragraph by Dan Fleming

From the beginning of Licking County's involvement with commemorating the 150th anniversary of the start of the Civil War, The Works* in Newark has played an integral part in the planning. Managing Director, Marcia Downes, stepped up early on to coordinate the efforts of every historical organization in the county that wanted to participate. She presided over monthly meetings where a year-long schedule of events was planned and advertised in newspapers, radio, the Licking County Convention and Visitors Bureau, and a hand-out publication. Nor did Marcia's efforts go unnoticed. She was chosen the "Historian of the Year" by the Licking County Historical Society at its annual meeting on July 8.

The Works itself sponsored wonderful programs throughout the year. Following is a short summary of its autumn events:

Oct. 15: The Works Harvest Festival "Celebrating the Civil War—Life Before Electricity." This annual event is sponsored by the Energy Cooperative this year and will feature Civil War reenactors roaming the courtyard, while sharing tales and demonstrating cooking and washing laundry in "the old days." Watch as a live sheep is shorn and the wool is turned into a shawl. Kids can decorate pumpkins, print Confederate bills, configure lightening bug circuits, and play Civil War era games. The museum and glass blowing shop will be open.

Oct. 16: Civil War Lecture: "Abraham Lincoln after 200 Years." Gerald Bazer, former Dean of Arts and Sciences at Owens Community College in Toledo, Ohio will explore how Lincoln rose from obscure and difficult beginnings to reach the White House, his role during the Civil War, views on slavery, and controversies surrounding his alleged abuses of civil liberties during the war. Free.

Nov. 4 – Jan. 9: "The Art of War" Gallery Exhibit. A free reception on Nov. 4 from 6-8 p.m. kicks off this exhibit centered on Newark inventor, Joseph Rider. His double action percussion revolver was used by the Remington Gun Company, which was a major weapon supplier in the Civil War. The gallery will also feature authentic Civil War artifacts, uniforms, period works of art and the Licking County battle flags (recreated).

Nov. 4 – Jan. 9: "150 Years of Trims & Treasures" is a display of beautifully decorated trees throughout the museum, courtesy of collectors and exhibit curators, Chuck Baughman and George Johnson. Original Thomas Nast Christmas prints and Civil War era ornaments will be displayed. 2nd floor shops will be transformed into vignettes of holidays past.

Nov. 5: Private Dinner & Lecture with Roy Marcot, historian of the Remington Gun Company. Tickets are $50 per person.

Nov. 13: Civil War Lecture, "An Echo of War, Gettysburg's Great 50 Year Reunion, 1913." Local Civil War historian, E. Chris Evans will conclude the Civil War lecture series with this presentation, discussing the 1913 reunion when both sides came together for the first time in peace.

Nov. 25: Holiday Traditions at The Works, "A Civil War Christmas." Get ready for holiday spirit by seeing how

Christmas was during the Civil War. The group, A'Chording to Tradition, will entertain with live dulcimer and guitar music. Kids may make holiday cards and watch science shows and glass blowing demonstrations. Chuck Baughman will speak on the history of holiday ornaments.

*The Works is a museum and interactive learning center located in downtown Newark, Ohio.

Grand Army of the Republic (G.A.R.) Posts in Licking County

Channel Post 188, Utica
Named for Capt. Aaron Channel, Co. E, 12th O.V.I.

Garfield Post 749, Jersey
Named for Col. James A. Garfield (later President), 42nd O.V.I.

Hamilton Post 311, Gratiot
Named for (1) William M. Hamilton, Co. B, 135th O.V.I.;

(2) Capt. Arthur T. Hamilton, 9th O.V.C.;

(3) Henry Hamilton, Co. G, 32nd O.V.I.; and

(4) Robert J. Hamilton, Co. G, 32nd O.V.I.

Ira P. French Post 693, Johnstown
Named for Ira P. French, Co. B, 76th O.V.I.

J. L. Francis Post 704, St. Louisville
Named for Capt. John L. Francis, Co. F, 135th O.V.I.

Josia Baird Post 653, Pataskala
Named for Pvt. Josia Baird, Co. D, 13th Missouri V. I. and 22nd O.V.I.

Lemert Post 71, Newark
Named for Capt. Thaddeus Lemert, Co. A, 76th O.V.I.

T. and J. Dill Post 463, Homer
Named for Brothers, Sgt. Thomas M. and 1st Lt. John A. Dill, both in Co. H, 76th O.V.I.

Z. P. Evans Post 668, Perryton
Named for Capt. Zebulon P. Evans, Co. A, 76th O.V.I.

Woman's Relief Corps, No. 45
(Auxiliary of Lemert Post 71, Newark)

Information provided by Larry Stevens, Newark, Ohio

APPENDIX 2

Major Battles of the 76th Ohio Volunteer Infantry

Fort Donelson, TN .... February 14-16, 1862

Shiloh, TN.. April 6-7, 1862

Corinth, MS (siege of) .... April 30-May 30, 1862

Milliken's Bend, LA..August 18, 1862

Chickasaw Bayou, MS............................ December 28-29, 1862

Arkansas Post, AR (Ft. Hindman)......................January 11, 1863

Vicksburg, MS (siege of) ....May 18-July 4, 1863

Canton, MS ....July 18, 1863

Jackson, MS .... July 9-16, 1863

Lookout Mountain, TN .... November 24, 1863

Mission Ridge, TN... November 25, 1863

Ringgold, GA... November 27, 1863

Resaca, GA...May 13-16, 1864

Dallas, GA.. May 25-June 4, 1864

Kenesaw Mountain, GA..June 9-30, 1864

Atlanta, GA (Hood's second sortie).........................July 22, 1864

Atlanta, GA (siege of) ....July 28-Sept. 1, 1864

Jonesboro, GA... August 31-Sept. 1, 1864

Lovejoy Station, GA ....September 2-6, 1864

Ship's Gap, GA .... October 16, 1864

Gadsen, AL.. October 26, 1864

Columbia, SC... February 16-17, 1865

Bentonville, NC .... March 19-21, 1865

Grand Review, Washington D.C. ....May 24, 1865

From: *Ohio at Vicksburg, Report of the Ohio Vicksburg Battlefield Commission,* by W. P. Gault, Sgt., Co. F, 78th O.V.I.

Appendix 3

Licking County Soldiers at Andersonville Prison, Georgia

Name..........................Company...........................Death Date

Alward, Alfred ....Co. B O.N.G. ....Sept 1, 1864

Anderson, Asbury ....Co. F O.N.G..........................Oct 7, 1864

Barnes, Thomas............Co. F O.N.G..........................Oct 7, 1864

Barstow, G. H...............Co. F O.N.G.........................Sept 9, 1864

Bell, Joseph..................Co. B 135th O.N.G. ....Sept 14, 1864

Benner, William A........Co. F 135th O.N.G...............Sept 8, 1864

Bogle, Holmes..............Co. B 135th O.N.G. .... Aug 16, 1864

Brookover, G. H...........Co. B 135th O.N.G. ....Sept 21, 1864

Carter, John R. ....Co. F 135th O.N.G.............Sept 14, 1864

Channell, Joel D...........Co. E 12th O.V.I.................Sept 17, 1864

Chapin, James A...........Co. F 135th O.N.G.............. Oct 28, 1864

Chapin, James, Sr.........Co. F 135th O.N.G.............Sept 14, 1864

Clark, J. R. ....Co. F 135th O.N.G.............Sept 15, 1864

Cooksey, William B. ....Co. B 135th O.N.G. ....Sept 14, 1864

Divan, Samuel..............Co. F 135th O.N.G................ Oct 1, 1864

Drake, John T. ....Co. F 135th O.N.G.............Sept 11, 1864

Ensley, William E.........Co. F 135th O.N.G............ Aug 16, 1864

Ewing, D. ....Co. D 135th O.N.G. .... Oct 29, 1864

Goff, Preston E.............21st O.V.I. .... Aug 15, 1864

Harvey, Charles............Co. E 76th O.V.I..

Hayner, B ....Co. A 135th O.N.G. ....Nov 6, 1864

Hayner, Enoch..............Co. A 12th O.V.I................. Aug 15, 1864

Hermon, R....................Co. F 135th O.N.G.............. Oct 11, 1864

Holmes, Wesley ....Co. F 135th O.N.G.............Sept 30, 1864

Hutchins, G. W.............Co. A 135th O.N.G. .... Oct 28, 1864

Jones, John ....Co G 45th O.V.I. .... Aug 12, 1864

Jones, S. D....................Co. F 135th O.N.G.............. Oct 10, 1864

Lemert, Thomas J.........Co. F 135th O.N.G.............Sept 14, 1864

Lewis, Nelson ....Co. B 135th O.N.G. ....

Lickliter, Henry............Co. B 135th O.N.G. .... Dec 14, 1864

Mark, J. ....Co. B 135th O.N.G. .... Oct 24, 1864

Martin, M. ....Co. B 135th O.N.G. .... Mar 6, 1865

McCloy, James.............Co. F 135th O.N.G.................................

McMillen, Charles ....

Miller, Samuel..............Co. F 135th O.N.G............Sept 14, 1864

Morris, E. J...................Co. F 135th O.N.G............. Aug 22, 1864

Morris, William H.........Co. F 135th O.N.G.............Sept 29, 1864

Myers, Loyd H. ....Co. B 135th O.N.G. ....Sept 1, 1864

Norman, G. L. ....Co. B 135th O.N.G. .... Dec 26, 1864

Ormsby, D. C. ....Co. C 135th O.N.G. ....Feb 1865

O'Sullivan, Timothy ....Co. E 76th O.V.I......................................

Palmer, Samuel ....Co. F 135th O.N.G............. Aug 27, 1864

Poor, A. M....................Co. B 135th O.N.G. ....Sept 12, 1864

Prior, Anthony M. ....Co. B 135th O.N.G. ....

Reader, George T..........Co. G 45th O.V.I. .... Aug 14, 1864

Rechell, John................Co. F 135th O.N.G............. Oct 11, 1864

Roberts, Leroy..............Co. B 135th O.N.G. ....

Sherman, Reuben ....Co. B 135th O.N.G. .... Oct 10, 1864

Sullivan, John...............Co. F 135th O.N.G..............Sept 9, 1864

Talbott, Rufus H...........Co. F 135th O.N.G............Sept 14, 1864

Van Kirk, George W. .....Co. B 135th O.N.G. .... Aug 18, 1864

Vinning, William H......H. Co. G 45th O.V.I. .... Jun 19, 1864

Williams, Joshua ....Co. E 12th O.V.I...................Sept 4, 1864

Wolf, Peter ....Co. B 135th O.N.G. .... Nov 11, 1864

Woodruff, J. M. ....Co. F 135th O.N.G............Sept 22, 1864

Carter, Charles C..........Co. F 135th O.N.G. (home) Feb 20, 1866

Please Note: This list may not be complete, especially for those who survived. It is based on the data given in *Report of the Great Re-Union of the Veteran Soldiers and Sailors of Ohio Held at Newark, July 22, 1878: under the Auspices of the Society of the Soldiers and Sailors of Licking County, Ohio*, by Charles D. Miller, 1879.

APPENDIX 4

Licking County Soldiers on the Steamship, Sultana

Name................................. Company .... Survived or Died

Allen, Morris..................... 95th O.V.I., Co. F.........................died

Anderson, James .... 1st Cavalry, Co. D ....survived

Evans, Edward W. .... 1st Cavalry, Co. D ....survived

Leese, Joseph .... 95th O.V.I., Co. F.........................died

Little, John .... 95th O.V.I., Co. F.........................died

Lugenbeal, William D. .... 135th O.N.G., Co. F...............survived
(early records show him as Daniel W. Lugenbeal)

McCarty, James W. .... 6th O.V.I., Co. D....................survived

Norris, Albert .... 76th O.V.I., Co. A ....survived

Roberts, Charles................ 12th O.V.I., Co. E ....died

Stone, James..................... 76th O.V.I., Co. D.................survived

Thomas, Thomas............... 76th O.V.I., Co. H.........................died

Thompson, James.............. 76th O.V.I., Co. A ....survived

Vanhorn, Burriss .... 95th O.V.I., Co. F...................survived

Wilcox, Marvin .... 95th O.V.I., Co. F.........................died

Wilson, Robert .... 95th O.V.I., Co. F...................survived

Yeisley, Emanuel Hush ..... 76th O.V.I., Co. G.................survived

SELECTED BIBLIOGRAPHY FOR FURTHER READING

Ancestry, Library edition. www.ancestrylibrary.com.

Brister, Judge E. M. P. *Centennial History of the City of Newark and Licking County*, Vol. 1. Chicago, IL: S. J. Clarke Publishing Co., 1909.

Bushnell, Rev. Henry. *The History of Granville, Licking County, Ohio*. Columbus, OH: Press of Hann & Adair, 1889.

Byer, Walter F. and Oscar F. Keydel, comp. *Deeds of Valor; How America's Heroes Won the Medal of Honor*, Vol. 1, 1901.

Civil War Documents, Series 147, Vol. 5: Adjutant General, Correspondence to the Governor and Adjutant General of Ohio July 5 – August 30, 1861 (at www.ohiohistory.org).

"Corner Stone of Newark's Memorial Temple Duly Laid," *Newark Advocate*, June 14, 1894.

Davis, William C. *Civil War Cookbook: A Unique Collection of Traditional Recipes and Anecdotes from the Civil War Period*. Philadelphia, PA: Courage Books, 1993.

Davis, William C. *A Taste for War: The Culinary History of the Blue and the Gray*. Mechanicsburg, PA: Stackpole Books, 2003.

French, Frank D. Correspondence with Minnie Hite Moody on file with the Licking County Genealogical Society.

Garrison, Webb. *A Treasury of Civil War Tales*. Nashville, TN: Rutledge Hill Press, 1988.

Graham, A. A. *History of Muskingum County, Ohio*. Columbus, OH: J. F. Everhart & Co., 1882.

Hill, N. N., Jr. *The History of Licking County, Ohio: Its Past and Present*. Newark, OH: A. A. Graham, 1881.

Jackson, Rita Richardson. *African-American Trailblazers, Licking County (1808-2008)*. Newark, OH: ATIR Pub., 2008.

Jackson, Rita Richardson. *Underground Railroad Stations*. Newark, Ohio: ATIR Pub., 2008.

Keirns, Aaron J., and Nathan J. Keirns. *Honoring the Veterans of Licking County, Ohio: An Illustrated History of Licking County's Military Heritage*. Howard, OH: Little River Publishing, 2009.

Livermore, Thomas L. *Numbers and Losses in the Civil War in America 1861-65*, 2002 repr.

"Major C. D. Miller Passes Away at 'Cedar Cliff' Saturday Night," *Newark Advocate*, July 28, 1898.

Markley, Bill. "History of the Licking County Infirmary," *Licking County Historical Society Quarterly*, Autumn 2010, Vol. 20, No. 4.

McRae, Bennie J., Jr. "United States Colored Soldiers, Sailors and Contrabands in America's Civil War." Web site at www.lwfaam.net/cw.

McTammany, Mary Jo. "The Rise and Fall of Federal Hill," *Clay County Line*, Oct. 26, 2005.

Miller, Charles D. *Report of the Great Reunion of the Veteran Soldiers and Sailors of Ohio held at Newark, July 22, 1878.* Newark, OH: Clark & Underwood, 1879.

Newark Advocate (hundreds of articles and advertisements from 1861-1864 -- few issues exist for 1865).

Ohio, Roster Commission. *Official Roster of the Soldiers of the State of Ohio in the War of the Rebellion, 1861-1866.* 12 v. Akron: Werner Co., 1886-1895.

Potter, Jerry O. *The Sultana Tragedy; America's Greatest Maritime Disaster.* Gretna, LA: Pelican Pub. Co., 1992.

Salecker, Gene Eric. *Disaster on the Mississippi; The Sultana Explosion, April 27, 1865.* Annapolis, MD: Naval Institute Pr., 1996.

Smythe, Brandt G. *Early Recollections of Newark.* Newark, OH: Thos. E. Hite Pubs., 1940.

Spaulding, Lily May and John Spaulding. *Civil War Recipes: Receipts from the Pages of Godey's Lady's Book.* U.S. Census on microfilm.

Weber, Elenore J., comp. *The Lemert-Montgomery Saga*, 1941.

Weber, Elenore. "Licking County Will Never Forget the Bravery of the Lemert Boys," *Newark Advocate*, June 25, 1980.

Bancroft, Ashley A., 5
Bancroft, Judge Samuel, 3, 5
banking, 106
Barnes, Thomas, 144
Barstow, G. H., 144
Bash, Henry, 116
Baughman, Chuck, 140, 141
Baughman Park, 128
Bazer, Gerald, 140
Beckwith, A. O., 120
Beckwith, Harry, 120
Beever, Morgan, 118
Bell, J. H., 117
Bell, Joseph, 144
Belt, William L., 116
Benner, William A., 144
Bentonville, Battle of, 143
Besse, Alden, 117
Bina, Mary Ann, 33
Black, Dr. James, 137
Blackburn, Lt. James, 59
Blazer, James, 116
bleeding (as a medical treatment), 99
Blue and Gray Central Ohio Civil War Roundtable, 135
Boggs, George H., 116
Bogle, Holmes, 144
Booth, John Wilkes, 84
Bostwick, Nathan, 116
Boudinot, Elisha, 81
Boudinot, Emma, 81-83
Boudinot, Henrietta Bundy, 81
Bourner, Sarah C., 119
Bricker, H., 116
Brister, Judge E. M. P., 121, 122
Brocius, Curly Bill, 131
Brookover, G. H., 144
Brown, Jay H., 67
Brown, William S., 67
Browne, James M., 116
Bryant's Minstrels, 45
Buchanan, President James, 3, 88
Buckeye Band, 122, 127
Buckingham, Lewis, 117
Buxton, Mervin, 118

Finegan, Michael S., 116
1st Arkansas Volunteer Infantry, 15, 60, 126
1st Ohio Volunteer Cavalry, 23, 72, 96, 126
flags, 13-15, 59-60, 120, 126, 140
Fletcher, J. P., 118
Ford's Theater, 84
Fort Donelson, Battle of, 12, 14, 76, 103, 143
Fort Hildeman, 68
Fort Sumter, xv, 9, 88
42nd Ohio Volunteer Infantry, 119
14th New Hampshire Volunteer Infantry, 130
4th of July celebration, 74
Francis, Captain John L., 119
Francis, Mary, 119
Fremont, John C., 3
French, Frank D., 60-61, 125
French, Captain Ira P., 59-60, 118
French, Truman B., 61
Fugitive Slave Law, 3
Fulton, R. S., 118

Gadsen, Battle of, 143
Galbraith, James, 135
G.A.R. (SEE: Grand Army of the Republic)
Gardner, Pvt. John W., 62-63
Gardner, W. H., 118
Garfield, President James A., 67, 70, 119, 125
Garfield Post #749, 119, 142
genealogical research, 130-131
General Order No. 11, 48
Gettysburg, Battle of, 109
Giffin, Charles B., 6
Glaze, J. H., 118
Goff, Preston E., 144
Grand Army of the Republic
    development of, 115
    Florida, operations in, 71
    founding of, 125
    Memorial Day started by, 134
    posts in Licking County, 63, 65, 67, 115-119, 122-124, 142
    reunions, 15, 129
Grand Review, 63, 143
Grant, General Ulysses S., 30, 76, 90
Granville Company, 10

Keene, Laura, 85
Kenesaw Mountain, Battle of, 143
Kibler, Col. Charles H., 41, 124
King, Samuel, 89
King, William, 117
Kingston, James R., 116
Klem (SEE: Clem)
Kline family, 55
knitting, 39-40
Knowlton, Levi, 116
Koos, John, 51
Koos's Confectionery, 51

Lacy, Dr. H. T., 103
Lamb, Emely J., 119
Lamb, Nelson M., 116
Land of Legend, xvi
Langdon, C. R., 118
Larimore, R. W., 118
Lattimer, J. W., 116
Laughery, John, 117
Leale, Dr. Charles Augustus, 85
Lee, General Robert E., 30, 109
Leese, Joseph A., 91, 146
Legg, Captain Andrew, 10, 41
Lemert, Beverly W., 66
Lemert, Charles C., 67
Lemert, Edward Leroy, 67
Lemert, Elizabeth Glasscock, 66, 68
Lemert family of Perryton, xiv
Lemert, George A., 67
Lemert, George L., 66-67
Lemert, George W., 67
Lemert, John Alexander, 67
Lemert, Laban, 66
Lemert, Minerva, 67
Lemert, Nathan Fleming, 67
Lemert, Orren, 66
Lemert Post #71, 116, 122-124, 128, 142
Lemert, Captain Thaddeus, 26, 62, 66, 68, 116
Lemert, Thomas Jefferson, 26, 67, 144
Lemmon, William, 118
Lennington, Thomas, 118
Lewis, Nelson, 144

McClelland, David, 116
McCloy, James, 145
McConnell, Ezra, 116
McCrum, Hester, 119
McCune, Eleanor, 137
McCune, Captain John H., 122, 137
McCune's Hardward, 10
McDougal, Captain Leonidas, 10, 17-18, 41, 55, 56, 60, 73, 121, 126
McDugall (SEE: McDougal)
McKinley, President William, 64, 65, 122
McKinney, Laura Maria, 65
McManus, Elizabeth, 119
McMaster, W. S., 117
McMillen, Charles, 145
McMillen, William W., 118
measles, 11
Medal of Honor, xvi, 64-65, 132, 137
medical advancements, 99-102
Meigs, M. C., 41
Memorial Day, 115, 125, 134-135
Memphis National Cemetery, 92, 93
Metzgar, Carrie, 12
Metzgar, John, 11-12
Metzger, Lt. John, 59
Mexico, War with, 72
Milburn, I. N., 117
militias, 9-10
Miller, Anna Gilman, 70
Miller, Brevet Major Charles Dana, 14, 70-71, 116, 125, 137
Miller, James, 70
Miller, Louisa, 119
Miller, Samuel, 145
Millikens Bend, Battle of, 76, 143
mills, 2
Mills, Warner, 117
Mission Ridge, Battle of, 14, 59, 143
Mississippi Marine Brigade, 78
Mitchell, Lucretia B., 63
Montgomery, Edward, 27
Montgomery, Henry A., 26
Montgomery, Mary Ellen Lemert, 26-27
Montgomery, W. C., 15
Montgomery, William, 59
Moore, David, 72, 113

Moore, Major David A. B., 10, 23-24, 72-73, 121
Moore, Moses, 72
Morey, Delano J., 132
Morgan, William D., 9
Morgan's Raiders, 75
Morris, E. J., 145
Morris, William H., 145
Murfreesboro, Battle of (SEE Stone River, Battle of)
Murphy, Joseph S., 118
museums, 124
Muskingum Home Guards, 26
Myers, Loyd H., 145

National Road, xiv, 2
Naylor, Helen, 119
Newark Advocate (newspaper), 9, 49-50, 74
Newark Depot, 113
Newark Militia, 17
Newkirk, Edward F., 116
newspapers, 4, 49-50
newsprint, scarcity of, 50
Newton & Keagy, 52
Nichols, Captain Edwin, 10, 41
95th Ohio Volunteer Infantry, 92, 94
97th Ohio Volunteer Infantry, 67
9th Ohio Volunteer Cavalry, 117
Norman, G. L., 145
Norris, Albert, 96, 125, 130, 146
Norris, Marilyn, 130, 131
North American (newspaper), 49
North Mountain Depot, Battle of, 30-31, 94, 119

O'Bannon, W. T., 116
O'Bannon, William H., 116
Octagon Mound, 65, 138
Ohio and Erie Canal, xiv, 1-2
Ohio Company, 74
Ohio Constitution (1851), 113
Ohio Historical Society, 15
Ohio National Guard, 65
Ohio State Anti-Slavery Convention, 5
150 Years of Trims & Treasures (exhibit), 140
101st Ohio Volunteer Infantry, 103
113th Ohio Volunteer Infantry, 126, 137

sewing machine, 34
Shellenberger, David, 133
Shellenberger, John S., 133
Sheridan Circle #6 (G.A.R. Auxiliary), 121, 122
Sheridan, General Philip, 109
Sherman, John, 11
Sherman, Reuben, 145
Sherman, Major General William Tecumseh, 11, 12, 62-63, 70, 88, 90, 125
Shiloh, Battle of, 76, 135, 143
Ship's Gap, Battle of, 143
Short, General John H., 126-127
Simmons, Harvey, 118
Sinnet, Alice, 105-106
Sinnet, Clara, 106-107
Sinnet, Dr. Edwin, 98, 103, 105-107
Sinnet, Sarah Wright, 105-106
Sinsabaugh, David A., 116
6th Wisconsin Infantry, 57
63rd Ohio Volunteer Infantry, 120
slavery, 3-4, 22, 74
Slough, Martin, 117
Smith, Lieutenant Colonel, 24
Smith, Ezra H., 116
Smith, General Kirby, 25
Smith, Miss M. B., 34
Smith, Peter, 113
Smoots, W. F., 116
Smucker, Isaac, 6, 113
socks, 39-40
Soldiers' Aid Society (Newark), 13, 20, 39, 41-42, 114, 120
    SEE ALSO: Young Ladies Soldiers' Aid Society (Granville)
Soldiers and Sailors Memorial Building, 65, 73, 121, 122-124, 126
Soldiers and Sailors of Licking County, 70-71, 128-129
Soldiers and Sailors Relief Commission, 124
Soldiers' Relief Committee, 6, 104, 113-114
Soliday, Romie, 119
Sons of Union Veterans of the Civil War, 128
South Mountain, Battle of, 64-65, 132
Spelman, George, 117
spies, 47-48
Squirrel Hunters, 25-29
Stafford, Maggie, 119
Stanbery, William, 3, 5
Standiford, E. R., 117

23rd Ohio Volunteer Infantry, 64

underground railroad, 6
Union Veteran Legion, 126, 128
United States Sanitary Commission, 36, 101
Universe (steamship), 14

Van Allen, J. L., 116
Van Atta, Miss M. M., 34
Vance, Captain J. B., 116, 122
Vandergriff, Ellen, 119
Vanhorn, Burriss, 91, 94, 146
Van Kirk, George W., 145
Veach, John F., 84-85
Vicksburg, Siege of, 143
Vinning, William H., 145
Voice of the People (newspaper), 74

Wagstaff, Dr. John O., 103
Waite, Chief Justice Morrison Remick, 90
Walker, Colonel Moses B., 74
War Democrats, 4
War of 1812, 79
Warner, Anne, 89
Warner, Luke K., 70
Warner, Brevet Brigadier General Willard, xv, 6, 15, 59, 70, 125
Warrenton Rifles, 108, 110
Washington, Martha, 80
Weaver, David, 118
Wehrle, Captain Joseph C., 41, 116
Westbrook, Captain Ulysses S., 30-31
White, Major, 84
White, Brevet Brigadier General Carr B., 85
White, Samuel, 3, 5
White, Wilson, 116
Whitney, William, 5
Wickham's Grove, 128
Wide Awakes, 60
Wilcox, Marvin, 91, 146
Wiley, Annie, 119
Williams, Adam, 118
Williams, Elizabeth, 78
Williams, George M., 116
Williams, Joshua, 145

Made in the USA
Charleston, SC
09 December 2011